DATE DUE

The Failure
of the NRA

THE NORTON ESSAYS IN AMERICAN HISTORY

Under the general editorship of
HAROLD M. HYMAN

William P. Hobby Professor of American History
Rice University

The Failure of
the NRA

Bernard Bellush

New York W · W · NORTON & COMPANY · INC ·

FIRST EDITION

Library of Congress Cataloging in Publication Data

Bellush, Bernard, 1917–
  The failure of the NRA.

  (The Norton essays in American history)
  Includes bibliographical references and index.
  1. United States. National Recovery Administration. I. Title.
HD3616.U46B44 1975   353.008′2   75–20318
ISBN 0–393–05548–5
ISBN 0–393–09223–2 pbk.

PRINTED IN THE UNITED STATES OF AMERICA

1 2 3 4 5 6 7 8 9

In Memory of
Edward C. Kirkland
Sidney H. Ditzion

Understanding, wisdom, and integrity for generations
of students, teachers, and scholars.

In Appreciation

ALWAYS THERE are others—friends and colleagues who help along the way, to encourage and to challenge one's intellectual efforts. Harold Hyman proved a judicious and rigorous editor, but with understanding and patience. Most welcome was the unique contribution of Esther Jacobson, whose editing skill and broad knowledge helped correct errors and strengthen concepts. Students at The City College of New York, and at the University of Utrecht in The Netherlands, were helpful with their questioning and challenging of my developing views on Franklin D. Roosevelt and the NRA. The devoted staff, outstanding resources, and calming environment of Baker Library at Dartmouth College made hardworking summers productive and attractive. And from France came Michele Gomy, whose devotion and loyalty kept the Bellush clan operating.

But most important, this writer is deeply indebted to Jewel Bellush, a self-effacing student of history and political science, and a stimulating teacher whose limitless horizon, provocative thinking, and incisive reactions continue to influence the writings of this colleague.

Those mentioned, and those unnamed, helped make this a more responsible work. And to them I am grateful. Its shortcomings remain mine alone.

Contents

Introduction

IN MANY introductory American-history courses the instructors, pressed for time as the end of the semester approaches, skimp on the New Deal. As a result, students tend to recall more vividly two earlier events of unusual stress and violence—Chicago's Haymarket riot of 1886 and the Pullman strike of 1894, involving Eugene V. Debs and the newly born American Railway Union. Few remember the great social and economic upheavals which swept the nation under the National Recovery Administration as part of a series of management-labor eruptions.

The advent of the post-Civil War industrial revolution in the United States facilitated a general decline over the years in the dignity of working men and women. With exceptions, they were forced to labor long hours, often for miserable wages, at dull, debilitating, and not infrequently dangerous tasks. Too many workers became mere pawns in the eyes of employers, the press, the clergy, the law, and the academy.

Only during our subsequent involvement in the First World War did industry and government deign, momentarily, to look upon a weakling labor movement as a legitimate and respected part of American democracy. But with the end of hostilities in November 1918, and on into the years of the Great Depression, industry and business spokesmen renewed their campaigns against workers who sought to organize or join independent trade unions, such as affiliates of the American Federation of Labor.

It was not uncommon for spies and agents provocateurs to be used to frustrate and crush union organizing drives. And if their efforts were not enough, state governors and other public officials cooperated by calling out state militia, National Guard units, and police to break strikes and, if necessary, shoot down peaceful pickets. Despite the Clayton Antitrust Act of the Wilson administration, which purportedly exempted striking trade unions from being deemed conspiracies in restraint of trade, federal judges issued sweeping injunctions in the 1920s against striking railroad, textile, steel, and other workers. Wherever working men and women turned, they seemed to find the major political, economic, and social forces arrayed against them.

Despite years of loyal and devoted service to employers, outspoken union members were often indiscriminately fired, without benefit of severance or unemployment-insurance payments. Child labor flourished, particularly among the spreading textile factories in the feudalism-ridden South. And many a steel worker labored for twelve hours a day, and twenty-four hours at a stretch when changing work shifts.

The New Era, otherwise known as the "roaring twenties," appeared to the unperceptive individual to be a period of limitless prosperity, signaling an end to cyclical depressions. Following the postwar economic collapse of 1920–21, there seemed to evolve an endless expansion in the automobile, radio, aircraft, rayon, and motion-picture industries, along with un-ending highway construction and suburban sprawl.

Superficially, working men and women appeared to enjoy the highest standards of living in their history. Actually, at the height of our much-vaunted prosperity, millions continued to live in poverty. By 1929, before the onset of hard times, one-third of our families received incomes which did not enable them to meet the minimum requirements of health and decency set by the United States Bureau of Labor Statistics.

During the "prosperous years" of the 1920s, there seemed to be no halt to increases in capitalization, new investment, and earnings. The public, however, was oblivious to a number of disturbing developments which had appeared by 1927—outright gambling in the stock market, a halt to expanded housing construction which facilitated an industry-wide recession, and a leveling off of automobile production which sparked a serious setback in allied industries.

A few months after respected industrialists and bankers affirmed, in February 1929, that the nation's economy was in a most fortunate situation, and that the momentum of prosperity was continuing unabated, there ensued a rapid decline in stock-market prices. This was followed by a gradual falling off of industrial production, and after October 1929, by the ushering in of the Great Depression.

Despite reiteration during the last months of 1929 by President Herbert Hoover and New York's Governor Franklin Delano Roosevelt that business was fundamentally sound, the nation's chief executive nevertheless felt obliged to appeal to industrialists to maintain wages and hasten new construction. A momentary improvement was immediately followed by renewed decline in commodity and farm prices. By June 1930, industry employed almost 15 percent fewer people than it had the previous year, and total wages had fallen some 20 percent. Between 1929 and 1932, the employment level dropped precipitously from 97.5 to 60.1 percent, real weekly earnings of those employed in manufacturing and mining generally fell 15 to 30 percent, the value of securities on the New York Stock Exchange contracted some 80 percent, the index of commodity prices dropped 40 percent, and payroll indices plummeted from 100.5 to the dismal figure of 35. Over half the population now subsisted on incomes below the minimum requirements for health and decency.

By the November 1932 presidential elections, the public was well aware of the impact of the economic decline. They did not need to be told that industrial production had fallen more than 50 percent, that new construction had all but ceased, or that unemployment was widespread. Hundreds of thousands of families had lost their life savings when more than a thousand banks closed their doors in 1930 and over two thousand in 1931. With Roosevelt's overwhelming victory at the presidential polls, the voters seemed to have declared that Herbert Hoover's extensive endeavors were inadequate, and to have mandated the new president to offer decisive leadership, if not radical measures. But above all, they appeared to be saying that speedy action was required. They had already been alerted to Roosevelt's readiness to break with tradition, when necessary. Refusing to await formal notification of his selection as the presidential nominee of the Democratic party, Roosevelt had flown at once from Albany, New York, to Chicago to deliver an acceptance address. In it, he stressed the need for the reconstruction of the nation's economy, and announced to the convention delegates, "I pledge you, I pledge myself, to a new deal for the American people."

Roosevelt was determined to reestablish a high level of economic activity, which he associated with the "prosperous" days of the New Era, and sought, through the National Industrial Recovery Act and its administrative arm, the National Recovery Administration, to stabilize the economy, increase the purchasing power of consumers, grant labor the right to organize and bargain collectively, and insure that capital earned a fair return.

Not until the advent of the New Deal did a nucleus of determined, courageous labor leaders begin to break the bonds of virtual servitude and gradually regain for many workers a semblance of human dignity. This change in the status of the American worker became evident when labor fought for and gained, ever so slowly, the right to organize and bargain collectively for shorter hours, for improved working conditions, for the abolition of child labor, for seniority among employees, for the right to strike as a last resort, for health and unemployment-insurance benefits, for pensions, vacations, and the upgrading of jobs.

The Failure
of the NRA

1

Industrial Recovery by Law

SHORTLY AFTER MIDNIGHT on June 16, 1933, a hundred days after it had been convened in special session by the newly inaugurated president, Franklin Delano Roosevelt, Congress adjourned, leaving a unique record of peacetime legislation. Later that same day, as Roosevelt signed the National Industrial Recovery Act (NIRA) in the presence of its smiling House and Senate proponents, he remarked to waiting newsmen, "History will probably record the NIRA as the most important and far-reaching legislation ever enacted by the American Congress." Outlining the Administration's policy under the act, FDR insisted that the NIRA would put millions of people back to work that summer, would enable them to buy more of the products of farms and factories, and would "start our business at a living rate again."

In his inaugural address, FDR had laid down the simple proposition that nobody was going to starve. It seemed to him, now, to be equally plain that no business which depended for its existence on paying less than living wages had any right to continue. The change in wage standards was to be made by an industrial covenant to which all employers would subscribe.

The President conceded that many good lawmakers had voted for this new charter with misgivings, particularly with reference to the initiatives accorded industry, but he promised to protect the public against "monopolies that restrain trade and price fixing which allows inordinate profits or unfairly high prices." In return, the Chief Executive expected the ten major industries which controlled the bulk of industrial employment to submit, within weeks, simple basic codes dealing with wages, hours, and methods necessary to prevent destruction of these standards by a nonconforming minority. By July, there would commence a great national movement back to work, the first result of the most important attempt of its kind in history.

Despite his selection of assorted, at times conflicting, advisers and working colleagues, Roosevelt made clear his overall devotion to the capitalist economy and to individual enterprise. But at the same time he displayed a flexibility and a willingness to learn, for he was prepared to resort to unusual experiments to stem the deepening chaos. He was much less intellectually committed to a precise goal of policy than were his early advisers among the Brain Trusters.[1] Influenced by such traditionalists and exponents of orthodox economics as Lewis W. Douglas, Jesse H. Jones, William H. Woodin, and Bernard M. Baruch, the President initiated severe governmental economies and revived the weakened banking system.

Shortly after his inaugural, the President had come under increasing pressure from various sources. Among these were economic planners in the business and academic world (some of the latter influenced by the Soviet experiment), proponents of large-scale public works, and advocates of federal intervention to enable workers to organize and bargain collectively through agents of their own choosing.

The antitrusters, or neo-Brandeisians, led by Supreme Court Justice Louis D. Brandeis and Professor Felix Frankfurter of the Harvard Law School, carried on the Wilsonian traditions of an earlier New Freedom as trust-busting liberals seeking to emanci-

1. The Brain Trusters, primarily university professors, were a group brought together by Samuel I. Rosenman to pepare policy papers and draft addresses for Roosevelt during his campaign for the presidency. See Elliot A. Rosen, "Roosevelt and the Brains Trust: An Historiographical Overview," *Political Science Quarterly,* 87 (December 1972), 531–63.

pate the economy from the evils associated with business monopolies. They favored a policy of business decentralization and enforced competitive behavior as the way to achieve prosperity. Monopolistic rigidity, they felt, had facilitated the depression through excessive profits, oversaving, and a failure of consumer purchasing power. The solution was vigorous antitrust prosecution, limits on the size of business, and controls over financing and competitive practices to insure reliance on free markets.

On the other hand, Henry I. Harriman, president of the United States Chamber of Commerce, believed that the Great Depression had been caused by overproduction, and urged, along with Gerard Swope, Baruch, and others, the adoption by the federal government of a policy of industrial self-regulation and the use of trade associations to eliminate destructive competition and to encourage national economic planning.

The cry for "planning," for a suspension of the antitrust laws, and for industrial codes to protect high-wage businessmen, had also arisen from such industries as oil, bituminous coal, cotton textiles, and garment-making, all plagued with chaotic conditions. Many retail trades urged government intervention to peg prices and remove the competitive advantages of the chain stores. Presidents John L. Lewis of the United Mine Workers (UMW) and Sidney Hillman of the Amalgamated Clothing Workers had pleaded with Congress and the President to stabilize their respective industries and to ease the worst effects of the depression through planning and a measure of industrial self-government.

Responding to similar thinking among many coal operators and Lewis' United Mine Workers, Senator James J. Davis and Representative Melville Clyde Kelly, both Republicans of Pennsylvania, had in January 1932 introduced a coal-stabilization bill which would relax the antitrust laws, establish a licensing commission, and encourage licensed producers to associate in order to control production and prices. This bill had good prospects for passage.

In the 1920s, trade associationists like Harriman had persistently proposed legalization of the work of these associations, which, under the sponsorship of Commerce Secretary Herbert Hoover, had attempted to eliminate destructive competition, maintain prices, and encourage national economic planning. Theodore Roosevelt and Herbert D. Croly had favored this approach during the Progressive era, and Woodrow Wilson had practiced it during the First World War. In the 1920s, Hoover had initiated more than two hundred codes of fair practice, under which companies shared product and market information, anticipating many aspects of the New Deal's NRA codes.

Economic planners of the New Nationalist vintage of an earlier Roosevelt rejected antitrust actions as anachronistic, for they accepted concentrations of economic power as inevitable in a modern society. But these planners were divided. Those on the political left, like Professor Rexford G. Tugwell, would have most of the planning done by the state or by organized non-business groups. Industrialists and pro-business planners, like Raymond Moley and Hugh S. Johnson, influenced by the War Industries Board of the First World War and by the associational activities of the 1920s, would rely upon enlightened business leadership through trade associations.

It was not unnatural for Roosevelt to think along the lines of "association." In the summer of 1922, Commerce Secretary Hoover and FDR had jointly founded the American Construction Council to prevent "unfair competition" within the construction industry, to stabilize and cartelize [2] the industry, and to develop planning through the imposition of codes of "ethics" and of "fair practice." The codes were the primary contribution of Hoover, while Roosevelt, as president of the Council, repeatedly denounced rugged individualism and profit-seeking by individuals. This trade association, like others in the 1920s, hoped to prevent such cutthroat practices as the use of inferior goods, depressed wages, and child labor. The organization of such associations was also a conscious endeavor to circumvent the antitrust laws.

2. A cartel is a syndicate or coalition of businesses formed to seek a monopoly within a specific trade or industry.

Roosevelt's experiences, however, taught him that voluntary self-regulation was inadequate to cope with unethical members who lowered wages and standards of production and resorted to child labor. By 1933, FDR had concluded that there would have to be some sort of "partnership with industry," which meant a voluntary setting of standards through trade associations exempt from antitrust laws, under some form of government supervision. He knew that Congressional progressives and Wilsonian liberals would howl, but he felt that they would eventually go along with his immediate objective of universal reemployment. Besides, politically they had nowhere else to go.

Twentieth-century progressives and liberals were committed, in varying degrees, to a sense of community, to the social good, to honest, responsible government, and to the interest of the consumer. They also included those who, since the turn of the century and beyond, had been challenging the inequities arising out of the economics of American society and had sought through political, governmental action at the city, the state, and then the federal level to bring about changes which would insure a better life. Rejecting radical extremism, progressives and liberals resorted, through the 1920s, to legal-judicial redress to achieve goals ranging from political reform to broad, national social justice for exploited women, children, and workers. A comparative few even spoke out vigorously on behalf of the black, the Indian, and other minorities.

New York Times, April 20, 26, 1933; Raymond Moley, *The First New Deal* (New York, 1966), 287–88; Daniel R. Fusfeld, *The Economic Thought of Franklin D. Roosevelt and the Origins of the New Deal* (New York, 1956), 102 ff.; Murray N. Rothbard, "Herbert Hoover and the Myth of Laissez-Faire," in Ronald Radosh and Murray N. Rothbard, eds., *A New History of Leviathan* (New York, 1972), 115; Gerald D. Nash, "Experiments in Industrial Mobilization: WIB and NRA," *Mid-America,* XLV (July 1963), 156–75. The reader who wishes to pursue more detailed research should consult the references listed at the ends of the subsections.

Hugo Black's Thirty-Hour Proposal

Within two weeks after his inaugural, FDR discussed priorities in his developing legislative program with his close adviser Moley, at this time assistant secretary of state. Chieftain of the original Brain Trust, until its demise in March 1933, Moley served the President as speech writer and receiver of callers on reform and policy proposals—as an outer-office filter. During this first month of his administration, Roosevelt became much too preoccupied with saving the banking system, shoring up agriculture, and initiating general relief plans. To be sure, the President was aware of the lack of knowledgeable planning and preparation for industrial-recovery legislation during the interregnum, and hence assigned Moley to collate and analyze various legislative proposals, and evolve them into one major plan. At the same time, Commerce Undersecretary John Dickinson, Senator Robert F. Wagner, Democrat of New York, and soft-spoken Labor Secretary Frances Perkins, the first female member of a presidential cabinet, were working along similar, though independent lines. Meanwhile, however, spokesmen for labor and social-welfare reform became restless in the absence of specific administrative proposals for industrial recovery and stabilization. The national administration thereupon lost the initiative in this field to a populist senator from the South. Hugo Black, Democrat of Alabama, was carrying on many of the traditions—in support of the poor farmer and in opposition to big business—of the challenging Southern Populist movement of the 1890s.

During the special session of Congress, Black's thirty-hour-work-week bill, introduced the previous December, made significant progress. Although the proposal contained no minimum-wage clauses (because of previous Supreme Court decisions and a traditional hostility by the American Federation of Labor [AF of L] on this issue), Black argued that a shorter work day would spread jobs, halt the expanding attack on labor standards, and increase the purchasing power of workers. His bill barred from interstate commerce articles produced in factories or mines which employed workers for more than thirty hours in a five-day week. Black's bill had the strong endorsement of the troubled, conservative leadership of the AF of L, which, at its Cincinnati convention in late November 1932, had begun to veer away from Samuel Gompers' historic policies of voluntarism and hostility to government intervention. The undramatic AF of L president, William Green, testifying before a Senate subcommittee in January 1933, was emboldened by the deteriorating economy to threaten general strikes to insure enactment of the bill.

On March 30, less than a month after FDR's inaugural, the Black bill was reported out favorably by the Senate Judiciary Committee. Except for a few hosiery employers, industry spokesmen denounced the bill as unconstitutional and bad economics. Debate, which began in earnest on April 3, indicated majority support. Confronted with the loss of legislative initiative in dealing with industrial recovery, and believing that the Black bill was not only unconstitutional but too rigid to be economically feasible, Roosevelt directed Senate Majority Leader Joseph T. Robinson, Democrat of Arkansas, to introduce an amendment raising the maximum hours permissible to thirty-six per week and eight per day. This Administration amendment was rejected 48 to 41 on April 5, and the following day the Senate adopted the original bill by a decisive 53-to-30 vote.

The President now thought it likely that Chairman William P. Connery, Jr., Democrat, of the House Labor Committee would call up his version of the Black bill at once, and he decided to move. On the one hand, he appointed a Cabinet committee headed by Labor Secretary Perkins to study the Black-Connery proposal and offer appropriate amendments to insure greater flexibility. At the same time, after consulting with Moley, who likewise viewed the bill as impractical and counterproductive, Roosevelt requested an alternative recovery measure without delay. There was also one last resort—to have the bill pigeonholed by a receptive Rules Committee in the House of Representatives.

On April 25, seven weeks after FDR's inaugural, Frances Perkins presented the findings of her Cabinet group before the House Labor Committee and threw industry leaders, some labor spokesmen, and conservative Administration members into consternation. Even the President shortly disowned her proposed amendments, as well as the bill itself. Recalling her recent experiences as industrial commissioner in New York when FDR was governor there, Perkins threw in her lot with the underconsumptionists, those who maintained that the key to business recovery was the expansion of mass purchasing power. She urged the adoption of the thirty-hour principle for most industries, with exceptions in emergencies, the creation of tripartite minimum-wage boards under supervision of the Department of Labor, and power to the Labor Secretary to restrict production and prevent cutthroat competition through the relaxation of antitrust laws and the creation of trade agreements.

On May 10, the House Labor Committee responded positively to the testimony of William Green, who rejected legislated minimum wages except for women and children, by unanimously accepting the Black-Connery bill and Green's proposal to grant workers the right to freely "belong to a bona fide labor organization and to bargain collectively for their wages through their own chosen representatives." Organized industry immediately rejected both the Black-Connery and the Perkins versions. At this time, the President took firm control and decided to push aggressively for an Administration substitute, for Roosevelt was determined to have the support of both industry and labor. The bill was then buried in the House Rules Committee. Consensus and moderation were the themes of the day.

Raymond Moley, *After Seven Years* (New York, 1939), 186; Frances Perkins, *The Roosevelt I Knew* (New York, 1946), 192–97; Moley, *The First New Deal*, 284, 287–88; Ellis Wayne Hawley, *The New Deal and the Problem of Monopoly: A Study in Economic Ambivalence* (Princeton, N. J., 1966), 21–23; Irving Bernstein, *Turbulent Years: A History of the American Worker, 1933–1941* (Boston, 1970), 26; *Thirty-Hour Bill,* hearings before House Labor

Committee on S. 158 and H.R. 4557 (73d Cong., 1st sess., April 25–
May 5, 1933), 66, 69; Irving Bernstein, *The New Deal Collective
Bargaining Policy* (Berkeley, Calif., 1950), 29–31.

A Fusion of Ideas

On the day in late April that Perkins testified before the
House Labor Committee, Moley unexpectedly encountered Hugh
S. Johnson and the latter's employer, veteran presidential adviser Bernard Baruch. Recalling the creativity and brilliance of
Johnson's powerful mind, appreciative of his administrative and
organizational contributions during the First World War, and
struck by his stimulating role as a speech writer and idea man
for FDR's presidential campaign, Moley invited Johnson to
study the plans for industrial stabilization and draw up a substitute for the Black-Connery bill. With the assent and advice
of Baruch, with whom Roosevelt was particularly anxious to
remain on friendly terms, Johnson hurried to an office adjacent
to Moley's feverishly to begin his new assignment. For the next
eighteen months, he was intimately involved with White House
developments.

The fifty-one-year-old Johnson had lived as a boy among
the Indians of the Oklahoma Territory, and had been a class-
mate of Douglas MacArthur at West Point, from which he
graduated in 1903. He was active in developing the plan for
the selective-service draft in 1917, and helped Baruch mobilize
American wartime industry through the War Industries Board.
In 1919 he resigned from the Army, and after working briefly
for Baruch, he assumed a managerial position with George N.
Peek at the Moline Plow Company. Upon leaving Peek, he re-
joined Baruch. During the 1932 presidential race, Johnson
worked closely with the Democratic campaign organization as
well as with the Brain Trust, as an expert on farm and business
policy.

The General was a heavyset man of medium height, "red
face, thick neck, hulking shoulders and barrel-chest," with a
jutting jaw and gravel voice that on first encounter helped con-

vey the impression of a gruff person. He was just about the "noisiest," "hardest-drinking" of the early New Dealers; his "majestic profanity" made him stand out in any group. He tended to inject himself needlessly into extremely complicated and highly sensitive negotiations, not infrequently blowing the whole situation sky-high. And yet he was, at heart, a sentimental and romantic individual who could be moved to tears by an opera scene or give way under persistent pressure.[3]

Johnson was a strong supporter of cooperation instead of competition within industry, and of the circumvention of antitrust laws by trade associations resorting to joint action. He believed, like Baruch and Moley, that antitrust laws had insured destructive competition, and was committed to establishing self-government in industry under some form of government supervision. Like Roosevelt, however, none of the three seriously regarded a new labor policy as relevant to recovery.

Faced with the task of creating an immediate substitute for the Black-Connery bill, Johnson labored with a variety of industrial-stabilization proposals and shortly presented Moley with a simple page-and-a-half document. It recommended suspending the antitrust laws, empowering the President to sanction agreements on labor and competitive business standards, and providing for federal licensing to secure compliance.

In the meantime, Senator Wagner had become restless in the absence of specific administrative proposals for industrial recovery. Two years earlier he had become interested in the negative aspects of the nation's antitrust tradition and had studied the views of Harriman and others on how to remedy some of these difficulties through industrial self-regulation and economic planning. The proposed National Economic Recovery Act drawn up by Dr. Harold G. Moulton of the Brookings Institution was particularly appealing. Wagner eventually recommended the lift-

3. Arthur M. Schlesinger, Jr., *The Age of Roosevelt* (3 vols., Boston, 1956–60), II, *The Coming of the New Deal,* 105–6; Bernstein, *Turbulent Years,* 43–44; Matthew Josephson, "The General," *New Yorker,* August 18, 1934, 20, 22; August 25, 1934, 28; September 1, 1934, 26–27.

ing of the American standard of living, and an attack on unemployment, by an economic general staff.

During the 1932 presidential campaign, it was Wagner, not Roosevelt, who demonstrated a consistent, forward-looking progressivism when he alerted the nation and his party's candidate to the need to plan for the rehousing of a third of the population. Since the memorable Triangle fire in New York City in 1911, Wagner had become increasingly recognized as a party spokesman for labor and social-welfare legislation, first in Albany and then in Washington. A longtime colleague of Alfred E. Smith and Roosevelt, he had urged upon the President a speedy infusion of massive public-works spending as a vital key to recovery.

It was, therefore, not unexpected that within weeks after his inaugural, Roosevelt should call upon the New York senator to draw up legislation relating to industrial stabilization and public works. For some time, a "Wagner group" of progressive bankers, industry and labor spokesmen, members of Congress, and others—among them Assistant Secretary of Agriculture Tugwell, Jerome N. Frank, brilliant general counsel to the Agriculture Adjustment Administration (AAA), Perkins, and Harold Moulton—had met to evolve a plan. A smaller drafting committee finally proposed self-regulation of business through trade associations, a public-works program, and a guarantee of the right of collective bargaining for organized labor.

On March 21, less than three weeks after his inaugural, in a message to Congress which dealt with relief proposals, the President had specifically recommended creation of a Civilian Conservation Corps (CCC) and a Federal Emergency Relief Administration (FERA). His third recommendation, a "broad public-works labor creating program," seemed to indicate victory for Wagner. However, FDR conceded that he had not reached a decision on a definite public-works proposal. Within days, Congress enabled the President to sign bills establishing the CCC and the FERA. But there were still no public-works or industrial-stabilization proposals.

J. Joseph Huthmacher, *Senator Robert F. Wagner and the Rise of Urban Liberalism* (New York, 1968), 135–38, 145–47; William E. Leuchtenberg, *Franklin D. Roosevelt and the New Deal* (New York, 1963), 52, 55; Hugh S. Johnson, *The Blue Eagle from Egg to Earth* (Garden City, N. Y., 1935), 193, 196–97; Bernstein, *New Deal Collective Bargaining Policy*, 31–32; Rexford G. Tugwell, *The Democratic Roosevelt* (Garden City, N. Y., 1957), 283–84; Donald R. Richberg, *The Rainbow* (Garden City, N. Y., 1936), 51; Rothbard, "Herbert Hoover and the Myth of Laissez-Faire," 119.

The White House Formulates a Bill

Hugh Johnson, meanwhile, had discovered that others too had been asked by the President to develop recommendations for achieving industrial stabilization and recovery. Before he completed the writing of his proposal, Johnson accepted Moley's suggestion that as a concession to the AF of L, he solicit the help of Donald R. Richberg in working out provisions relating to labor's rights. Richberg had already drafted a collective-bargaining statement, based upon his earlier experience with the Railway Labor Act of 1926 and the Norris–La Guardia Anti-Injunction Act of 1932, which emphasized freedom of association in the designation of bargaining representatives. In an effort to blunt the Congressional strength of the labor-endorsed Black-Connery bill, and not because he deemed labor policy a key to recovery, Johnson permitted Richberg to develop this labor clause. It was soon apparent that Richberg generally agreed with Moley and Johnson.

In testimony before the Senate Finance Committee, shortly before Roosevelt's inaugural in March, Richberg had expressed well-developed ideas about industrial recovery. He believed in business-government planning to increase consumer consumption through higher wages and lower prices, rather than in cutting production and raising prices. He endorsed self-government in industry, supporting the creation of industrial councils composed of representatives of managers, investors, and workers to insure a "legal limitation on profit-making in the essential industries," and the encouragement and protection of the rights of labor. Earlier, he had worked with progressive Senators Robert M. La Follette, Jr., Republican of Wisconsin, Edward P. Costigan, Democrat of Colorado, and Bronson M. Cutting, Republican of New Mexico, in the formation of a public-works bill to facilitate recovery through priming the pump.

When Johnson expressed dissatisfaction about confusing and conflicting proposals on industrial stabilization, Moley helped convene a meeting in the White House, on May 10, which included the President, Johnson, Dickinson, Perkins, Richberg, Wagner, Douglas, and some Congressional leaders. Just before the White House conference began, the House Labor Committee approved the thirty-hour-work-week proposal of Senator Black, placing additional pressure on Roosevelt. When the White House group failed to reach a compromise after two hours of discussion, the President directed them to shut themselves in a room, iron out the differences, and bring him a bill on which they could all agree. Despite his disinterest in collective bargaining, Roosevelt endorsed the general consensus for such legislation, feeling that it would insure him the support of labor and be an excellent start for a successful omnibus approach. A drafting committee, which at first included Douglas, Johnson, Wagner, Richberg, Perkins, Tugwell, and Dickinson, but finally ended up without the latter three, hammered out a crazy patchwork quilt of conflicting ideas. Johnson's page-and-a-half proposal had now evolved into a lengthy document. As an adherent of fiscal orthodoxy, Douglas unsuccessfully sought to overcome Wagner's insistence on inclusion of a 3.3-billion-dollar public-works program. And then Wagner threatened to withdraw from the group should his colleagues accede to the pressure of a visiting delegation from the National Association of Manufacturers (NAM) to delete from the proposed draft Section 7a, affirming labor's right to organize and to bargain collectively.

Wagner gained his point with respect to Section 7a, but he did yield to Johnson's insistence that Congress delegate many of its traditional prerogatives to the President. Tremendous legislative powers relating to resource allocation, production, organization, wage and hour scales, and relations between labor and management, all adding up to administrative control of the economic processes of the nation, were to be removed from the purview of Congress and handed over to the Chief Executive. Johnson won out over Wagner when he insisted that "codes of fair competition," developed by the President or his spokesman, would apply to all industries involved in interstate commerce, not just to a limited number like the steel and automobile industries.

The omnibus compromise—the proposed National Industrial Recovery Act (NIRA)—finally emerged on the floor of Congress on May 17, less than eleven weeks after the President's inaugural. It sought to satisfy advocates of social reform, public works, trust-busting, organized labor, self-regulation, state capitalism, and economic planning. In it were found all sorts of strands of social and economic reform, conservative provisions for the protection of capitalism, and a legitimization of the trade-association concept of the 1920s. Under Title I of the proposed legislation a national emergency was declared, which justified a partial suspension of the antitrust laws for two years. Title I showed the impact of national-planning advocates, for it provided that members of an industry could, with the collaboration of the government, draw up codes applicable to the entire industry that would have the power of law when approved by the President, being enforceable by the courts. Wide powers were delegated to the President, who could approve or disapprove a code, amend or amplify it, and even impose one where there was no agreement within an industry. The President was also empowered to license businesses; this procedure would force the minority of recalcitrant entrepreneurs into line, since shipments in interstate commerce by unlicensed establishments, were banned.

Labor was given Sections 7a, b, and c, which accorded employees the right to organize and bargain collectively through representatives of their own choosing, and the freedom to join a labor organization, and required employer compliance with provisions for maximum hours of labor, minimum rates of pay, and other working conditions approved by the President. The Chief Executive had the responsibility of insuring that the codes did not promote monopoly or oppress the small producer.

Title II would engender little dispute in Congress. It gave recognition to public-works advocates, for it authorized the President to create an emergency Public Works Administration (PWA) with authority to expend up to 3.3 billion dollars, both directly and through the Reconstruction Finance Corporation (RFC), on highways, dams, federal buildings, and other undertakings, even including naval construction.

Moley, *After Seven Years,* 187–88; Johnson, *The Blue Eagle,* 201–3; Richberg, *The Rainbow,* 106–7; Thomas E. Vadney, *The Wayward Liberal: A Political Biography of Donald Richberg* (Lexington, Ky., 1970), 115–17; Huthmacher, *Senator Robert F. Wagner,* 147–48; Tugwell, *The Democratic Roosevelt,* 284; the text of Title I may be found in Leverett S. Lyon et al., *The National Recovery Administration, Analysis and Appraisal* (Washington, D. C., 1935), 889–99.

Lobbying on the NIRA

In the process of laying the groundwork for public and Congressional support of the forthcoming industrial-recovery proposal, FDR remarked at a Chamber of Commerce meeting on May 4 that it was "human nature to view a problem in terms of the particular experience and interest of the company or the business with which one is personally associated. . . . It is ultimately of little avail to any of you to be temporarily prosperous while others are permanently depressed." [4]

The Chief Executive's second "fireside chat," three days later, dealt with a "partnership" between private industry and

4. Samuel I. Rosenman, ed., *The Public Papers and Addresses of Franklin D. Roosevelt* (13 vols., New York, 1938–50), II, *The Year of Crisis, 1933,* 157.

government. FDR appealed to the American public to understand and support his concept of partnership, insisting that it was wholly wrong to regard the measures adopted by the New Deal Congress as "government control of farming, industry and transportation."

In his message to Congress on May 17, recommending immediate action on his proposed industrial-recovery bill, the President urged the lawmakers to establish the necessary machinery for "a great cooperative movement throughout all industry in order to obtain wide reemployment, to shorten the working week, to pay a decent wage for the shorter week and to prevent unfair competition and disastrous overproduction."

The President knew by now that industry would not be averse to the major thrust of his industrial-recovery program, for he had learned from Harriman that the "psychology of the country is now ready for self-regulation of industry with government approval of agreements reached either within or without trade conferences." And why should industry object? The new recovery measure was substantially what industry had been asking for since being confronted with Senator Black's proposal.

As Senator Wagner introduced the Administration's industrial-recovery bill, he realized that it would come under strident attack from both sides of the chamber, by rural progressives, antitrusters, and spokesmen for small-business liberals and the competitive tradition. They feared that the suspension of antitrust laws, and the concession to business of the rights of self-government, might result in price-fixing and production-limitation agreements. The New York senator, who normally found himself collaborating with other progressives, was soon part of a strange coalition.

The three-day hearings on the NIRA proposal before the House Ways and Means Committee, which began on May 18, were marked by an absence of debate or hostility between industry and labor representatives. Spokesmen for the Chamber of Commerce and the AF of L had apparently concluded a private agreement whereby the former would accept the labor section while the latter would accede to the trade-association features. The National Association of Manufacturers, which had refused to become a party to this agreement, withheld its blasts for another day.

William Green appeared before the House Committee on May 19; he sought to buttress workers' protection against employer restrictions by recommending insertion in Section 7a, of a passage taken largely verbatim from the Norris–La Guardia Anti-Injunction Act of 1932; "and shall be free from the interference, restraint, or coercion of employers of labor, or their agents, in the designation of such representatives or in self-organization or in other concerted activities for the purpose of collective bargaining or other mutual aid or protection."

Green also suggested that in the next clause, "company union"—by which he meant an association sponsored, financed, and controlled by the company or corporation involved—be substituted for "organization," so that the passage would read: "that no employee and no one seeking employment shall be required as a condition of employment to join a company union, or to refrain from joining a labor organization of his own choosing." The objective was to safeguard the closed shop, where a majority vote committed all the workers of a particular enterprise to being represented by an independent union, to which all were obliged to pay dues.

Suddenly confronted with the possibility of achieving through industry-wide codes their long-term goals with respect to collective bargaining and the limitation of work hours, Green and most labor leaders were willing to accept, in exchange, price-fixing by business. They seemed to be unaware of its potentially negative impact upon consumers, many of them trade-union members. In the meantime, Richberg provided additional ammunition to suspicious progressives when he made the admission to the House Committee, subsequently affirmed by businessman Harriman, that enactment of the NIRA proposal might well encourage manufacturers to fix prices in the manner of European cartels. And this kind of price-fixing was exactly what the National Association of Manufacturers projected in its model code, which it issued on May 31.

National Industrial Recovery, hearings before Senate Finance Committee on S. 1712 and H.R. 5755 (73d Cong., 1st sess., May 22, 1933), 1–2; Rosenman, ed., *The Year of Crisis,* 157; Bernstein, *New Deal Collective Bargaining Policy,* 34; Bernstein, *Turbulent Years,* 32; Henry I. Harriman to FDR, May 11, 1933, Franklin D. Roosevelt Papers, Franklin D. Roosevelt Library, Official File 466, hereafter cited as Roosevelt Papers, OF 466; *Unemployed,* hearings before House Ways and Means Committee on H.R. 5664 (73d Cong., 1st sess., May 18–20, 1933), 91–92, 117–42.

Progressives Indict the NIRA Proposal

On May 23, a week after the bill was introduced to Congress, the House Ways and Means Committee reported it favorably, including the Green amendments. The proposal, however, did not go through smoothly. In fact, Administration forces narrowly escaped being upset when House leaders managed, by the barest of margins, to adopt a special rule which limited floor amendments to those proposed by the House Committee, and restricted debate drastically. This rule had been used by Administration leaders often in the lower house during this special session. The near revolt followed hard upon the disclosure in a Senate subcommittee that millionaire J. P. Morgan and his many business partners had avoided payment of any income tax for the years 1931 and 1932, because of a loophole in the existing law. Eighty-two Democrats and five Farmer-Laborites deserted the President on the issue of drastically restricting debate, and they barely lost, 194 to 213. On May 26, after a two-day debate, the House overwhelmingly adopted the industrial-recovery bill, 325 to 76.

On June 7, three weeks after the bill was first introduced to Congress, the Senate Finance Committee submitted its revised version of H.R. 5755, the National Industrial Recovery Bill, to the full Senate. It seemed inevitable that a Congressional conference committee would have to eliminate the radical differences between the strictly Administration measure passed in the House and the much-altered bill now before the Senate. In a prepared address to his colleagues, Wagner insisted that antitrust laws had not only failed to check the constant increase in the size of business units and the concentration of economic power in the hands of a relatively few, but had been invoked most successfully in litigation to curb the laborer and the small businessmen. He sought to reassure his doubting progressive colleagues that no code would be approved which discriminated against small enterprise. Instead, he confused them when he insisted that the measure would bring about the fulfillment of the original objectives behind antitrust legislation.

Wagner was sensitive to expected attacks on the constitutionality of the bill, and speaking for many urban progressives, he cited Supreme Court decisions which he felt had condemned discriminatory and deceptive business practices. He fell back upon cases dating from 1887 to bulwark his contention that in the existing crisis of reduced wages, crime, and immorality any comprehensive scheme for restoring wage payments was related to the health, safety, and morals of the people. Wagner felt that the dissents of Justice Brandeis, with his ominous warnings against the arrest of social and economic experiments, were the harbingers of future court decisions. In his concluding remarks, the New York senator placed too much reliance on one man as he maintained that the bill would be administered "with the humane sympathies, level-headed judgement, and splendid valor which the President has shown in all his actions."

Within moments William E. Borah, the veteran Republican and old-line progressive from Idaho, was on his feet, engaging Wagner in a long series of cogent exchanges which set the stage for the most heated controversy of the eventful Hundred Days at the start of Roosevelt's first administration. Speaking for rural progressives and antitrusters, Borah pinpointed those provisions of Title I which set aside the antitrust laws for two years. He felt that they would facilitate the blossoming of trusts and combines, "but we are not to call them such," and would enable the larger interests to dominate the small businessmen. Borah, and others who endorsed his viewpoint, insisted that well-organized and experienced industrial spokesmen would quickly dominate the code-making process, and use it to the detriment of the consumer and the laborer. The result would be increased concentration, rather than more equitable distribution, of wealth. There was nothing in the bill to indicate what was "fair competition," and no rule to protect the consumer. Congress, insisted Borah, was being asked to abdicate to a president who would be unable to supervise the details of thousands of businesses, and therefore would delegate authority to one or more individuals, unknown to Congress; pass upon the question of fair competition, without any guide or direction from the law-making power of the United States. Borah had made his point.

Immediately, the mercurial, immodest populist from Louisiana, Democrat Huey P. Long, took the floor, and held it for more than two hours in a mini-filibuster against Title I. The Kingfish, as he was called by newsmen, walked about, waved his arms, tousled his red hair, and went through his "usual gyrations." With biting sarcasm and homey illustrations, he lamented the President's decision to sidetrack Black's thirty-hour-work-week proposal. Title I, he reminded his embarrassed fellow Democrats, was a repudiation of the party platform adopted at the Chicago nominating convention the previous year, which promised a "strengthening and impartial enforcement of the antitrust law." Instead of passing laws of a specific nature, Congress was now authorizing the President to suspend the Constitution and the antitrust laws. Opposing the delegation of legislative power to the Chief Executive, Long insisted that Congress should be the body to approve a code or codes of fair competition, as cited in the proposed bill. "If Senators want to shift hours of labor and keep production up with consumption, there is a way to do it without enacting into law any such monstrosity as this."

Long continued his attack by insisting that this was the most tyrannical law he had seen proposed since he had joined the United States Senate. "Every fault of Socialism is found in this bill, without one of its virtues. . . . Worse than anything proposed under the soviet." He conceded that the bill would put people back to work: "There won't be any unemployment at all. They'll all be in jail for violating this infernal thing."

When Long lamented his inability to get along of late with the President and his administration, arch-conservative Republican David Reed of Pennsylvania interrupted to ask what the trouble had been. The lightning reply of the quixotic senator from Louisiana was, "One trouble has been that the administration has been for too many things that the Senator from Pennsylvania stood for." Although laughter rang through the chamber, progressive Democrats and Republicans agreed with the overall thrust of Long's indictment.[5] Long was clearly determined to strike out the "iniquitous" Title I, and yet his final vote would surprise all.

Many progressives, such as Montana's Burton K. Wheeler, a Democrat, had a number of reservations, but were prepared at first to submerge them in support of the President. Huey Long, however, continued to attack Title I during subsequent debate. He feared that it would ruin labor, destroy competition, and increase the cost of goods to the consumer. He lamented the fact that Wagner, who had been fighting for labor and social legislation all his life, had joined the business crowd "across the mahogany table." He went further to denounce the rumored appointment of Johnson as administrator of the act. The former general had been a close associate of Baruch, who—Long insisted—had consistently exerted negative influences on the Wilson and Hoover administrations. This was the same Baruch who had supported a national sales tax proposal at the height of the depression, and who allied himself with some of the most conservative elements in the Democratic party.

5. Debates of June 7 and 8, 1933, *Congressional Record* (73d Cong., 1st sess.), LXXVII, 5174–84, 5238–53, 5307–8; *New York Times,* June 8, 1933.

It was the alertness and parliamentary wizardry of progressive Republican George W. Norris of Nebraska that insured full debate and spotlighting of the amendment, introduced by Senator Bennett Champ Clark, conservative Democrat from Missouri, which sought to circumvent the basic intent of Section 7a. Clark's amendment stated that "nothing in this title shall be construed to compel a change in existing satisfactory relationships between the employees and employers of any particular plant, firm or corporation." Norris was joined in the fight against the proviso by Costigan, Wheeler, Long, Democrat Homer Bone of Washington, Wagner, and Republican Arthur Robinson of Indiana. All attacked the Clark amendment as a direct blow at organized labor, legalizing employer-dominated company unions, facilitating the organization by employers of company unions, and condoning the yellow-dog contract.[6] Eventually the Senate deleted the Clark amendment by a vote of 46 to 31; the majority seemed to be saying that in 1933 it was prepared to support the independent trade union movement as against company unions.

National Industrial Recovery, hearings before House Ways and Means Committee on H.R. 5664 (73d Cong., 1st sess., May 18–20, 1933) 122, 137; Bernstein, *Turbulent Years,* 32; *New York Times,* June 8, 9, 1933.

Progressives Lose on the Final Bill

During tiresome day and night sessions, sometimes totaling thirteen hours at a stretch, presidential forces were generally in command as voting proceeded on amendments. Borah's amendment to prohibit any code of fair competition from permitting

6. A yellow-dog contract was a written contract, signed by an employee as a condition of obtaining employment, in which he agreed that he would not join a union or, if he was a union member, that he would dissociate himself from it. Further, he would not quit without giving sufficient notice to his employer to enable him to hire someone to take his place. The employee also generally agreed in advance to accept such conditions of labor as the employer might decide upon. These provisions took away from the worker the right to have anything to say about any conditions of his employment.

"combinations in restraint of trade, price fixing or other monopolistic practices" was approved. La Follette's proposal to publish corporate and personal income-tax returns was accepted by a 2-to-1 vote. With a number of similar strengthening amendments, the final bill received the overwhelming endorsement of the antitrusters and the Senate on June 9, originally by a vote of 57 to 25. Although both Black and Long had voted against Title I on an earlier ballot, only four conservative Democrats joined twenty Republicans and Long to oppose the entire bill. Ten independent or progressive GOP members and Farmer-Laborite Henrik Shipstead of Minnesota joined forty-six Democrats as the affirmative bloc.

Upon completion of the roll call, Huey Long asked Vice President John Nance Garner, of Texas, who was chairing the session, "How should a vote be cast when a Senator is half against and half in favor of a bill?" An irritated Vice President replied, "The Senator would have to cut himself in two, which would be difficult to do." At that moment, in spite of his marathon denunciations of Title I, Long switched his vote to support the bill, the final tally being 58 to 24.[7]

The results were immediately referred to a conference committee, to facilitate the development of acceptable compromises and to enable tired legislators to adjourn the special session and return home. Unfortunately for the antitrusters in the upper chamber, those designated as Senate managers of the conference committee—Democrats Pat Harrison of Mississippi, William H. King of Utah, and Walter F. George of Georgia—were more attuned to the conservative wishes of a President responding to protesting industry than to the desires of the majority which had pushed through a number of vital amendments. The result was a conference report which removed the specific prohibitions of "price fixing or other monopolistic practices," and revised the La Follette amendment so drastically that it became meaningless.

Within twenty-four hours of the original Senate approval, the House ratified the conference report and disposed of all other

7. *Congressional Record* (73d Cong., 1st sess.), LXXVII, 5424.

legislation before it. The pressure was now on the Senate to speed adjournment. But not until June 13, and after five hours of heated discussion, did the Senate act upon the conference report.

Senators Wheeler, Long, Borah, Black, and Cutting immediately denounced the vital concessions made to House conferees. Not a recognized progressive from either side of the chamber supported Harrison or a harassed Wagner as they sought to defend the conference report. Borah insisted that the revised bill would permit combinations in restraint of trade as well as price-fixing. Wheeler rejected Wagner's assurances that the organization to be set up under Johnson would stop monopolistic practices, and maintained rather that the bill would permit the members of an industry to agree upon prices and arrange their own codes.

Black of Alabama now rose for the first time during these intensive debates, and made telling points against Wagner and the conference report. He recalled the objectives of his thirty-hour-work-week-bill—to abolish sweatshops, reduce hours of labor, and increase wages so that purchasing power might keep pace with expanded production—and declared that he preferred to reach these objectives by direct legislative means rather than by turning over the matter to representatives of those industries which were themselves the chief offenders. Touching upon an argument advanced by Tugwell and by the earlier Southern Populists, Black indicated that he saw no advantage to raising the salary of the wage earner unless, at the same time, Congress decreased the exorbitant earnings of capital. No serious rebuttal was offered by Black's colleagues.

When Wagner replied that the original Borah amendment, if retained, might prohibit agreements establishing minimum wages, because that was part of price-fixing, Black cut the ground from under the New Yorker by insisting that the conference committee could have amended the Borah proviso to insure that it would not apply to combinations fixing minimum wages or the hours of labor. Wheeler, Cutting, and La Follette then lamented the practice of appointing to conference committees members who did not make any serious attempt to preserve the integrity of a bill's amendments.

When La Follette moved to recommit the report to the conference committee, the chair ruled that this was impossible because the House had already approved it. The only parliamentary alternatives, at that moment, were to approve or to reject the report. On the motion to accept the conference report, Wagner found himself deserted by many of his progressive colleagues. Four days after they had voted for the original industrial-recovery bill, with amendments, eighteen progressives and antitrusters swung over to the opposition, along with three colleagues who had previously been recorded as not voting. In contrast, those remaining in the affirmative were now joined by two who had previously rejected the bill, along with six others who had not voted on the original proposal. Two who had previously voted yes, and four who had voted no, were now recorded as not voting on the conference report. The President was sustained, in this instance, by a close, conservatively oriented vote of 46 to 39.

Debates of June 9 and 13, 1933, *Congressional Record* (73d Cong., 1st sess.), LXXVII, 5424, 5608, 5861; T. Harry Williams, *Huey Long* (New York, 1969), 635; *New York Times,* June 10, 14, 1933.

The NIRA as Passed

The President made it clear that of the alternatives offered him by the NIRA, he was going to rely on the initiative of trade and industrial associations to formulate industry-wide codes. And General Hugh S. Johnson, who on June 16 was appointed administrator of the National Recovery Administration (NRA)—the name given to the administrative agency which was to implement Title I of the NIRA—concluded that he would resort to the voluntary method of code initiation and not invoke the licensing provisions of the Act. The General feared that the NIRA, which greatly expanded the role of a peacetime federal government in resource allocation, production organization, the determination of wage and hour scales, and the relations between labor and management, might be unconstitutional.

In its enacted form, the NIRA contained three titles, the third dealing with capital-stock and excess-profits taxes to help finance the public works which were authorized in Title II. The most discussed portion of the Act was Title I. The first section contained a general declaration of policy—to promote cooperative action, eliminate unfair practices, increase purchasing power, expand production, reduce unemployment, and conserve natural resources—but did not specify how these objectives were to be achieved. The second section imposed a limit of two years, and authorized the President to designate or create appropriate administrative agencies, to appoint officers and employees without regard to civil-service laws, and to delegate any or all of his functions and powers under this act to such agents as he might designate or appoint. Subsequent sections established the rules for code-making. Section 3 assigned the President authority to approve for trades and industries equitable, representative codes which did not promote monopolies or monopolistic practices. He could add or delete segments or impose entirely new codes.

Little was said about the provisions to be contained in the codes, except for labor standards as provided in Section 7, including—in Section 7a—the outlawing of yellow-dog contracts and a guarantee to employees of the right to organize and bargain collectively through representatives of their own choosing. Section 4a authorized the President to enter into voluntary agreements if they would help accomplish the purposes of the law. It would be under this section that Roosevelt would promulgate the President's Reemployment Agreement, popularly called the "blanket code," for which the Blue Eagle emblem would be invented. Section 4b contained the controversial licensing provision, which gave the President the power of life or death over business enterprises, but which he would never use. It had been bitterly attacked as the most extraordinary extension of presidential power in American history. Section 5 exempted the codes from antitrust laws; Section 8 provided that they should not conflict with provisions of the Agricultural Adjustment Act; and Section 10 authorized the Chief Executive to remake in any way any code at any time during the life of the law.

Initial Reaction to the NIRA

It should have been apparent to Roosevelt, as it was to Tugwell and others, that Senate progressives had rejected Title I of the NIRA in its final version. They were perplexed by its indiscriminate fusion of ideas for economic recovery and social reconstruction. They were uncertain as to the direction in which the New Deal was heading and fearful as to who would be controlling the new institutions they were creating. While anxious to cooperate with the President in facilitating a period of social and cultural transformation, they did not want to help establish large planning organizations for industry in which big business and management would co-opt the political decision-making system.

Old-line labor spokesmen welcomed the NIRA, for with it the AF of L seemed to have gained most of its legislative demands. Besides the prospect of mass organization and collective bargaining offered by Section 7a, the Act apparently presented the possibility of shorter hours through codes, and of increased employment through a public-works program. As Gompers had indiscriminately done with the Clayton Antitrust Act some two decades earlier, Green hailed Section 7a, calling it a "Magna Charta" for labor. An expansive Lewis compared it with the Emancipation Proclamation.

By contrast, Socialist party leader Norman Thomas had, from the start, opposed the ideology and programs behind the earlier recommendations of Swope, Harriman, and others which led to this omnibus enactment. According to Thomas, these proposals were "a complete denial of the bases of the old capitalism, but . . . set up instead a capitalist syndicalism still operated for profit, a scheme which is in essence fascist." The plans of Swope and others were "vitally concerned . . . to preserve private

property for power and private profit," even though they cut
the ground from under old-style competitive capitalism.

Thomas did concede in 1933 that Roosevelt was far in advance of his own Democratic party, and welcomed Section 7a
for the encouragement it afforded workers to organize. While
soon fearing that Roosevelt's aim was to have the unions become
mere appendages of his administration in Washington, Thomas
nevertheless noted that for the first time in American history,
collective bargaining was given sanction by the federal government. And he foresaw the possibility that an organized labor
movement, independent of the New Deal, might yet achieve unprecedented power in American life.

However, Thomas went on to offer the gravest reservations
as he lambasted the overall direction of the NIRA. While not
characterizing the legislation in particular, or the New Deal in
general, as clearly fascist, as did the Communist party and its
leadership, Thomas continued to recognize certain parallels between the economics of state capitalism and of fascism. He
feared that the NIRA, with an inevitable bias toward large-scale
business, had the potential of causing movement in a fascist
direction.

Three decades later, New Deal historian William E. Leuchtenberg underscored Thomas' major indictment when he maintained
that with the adoption of the NIRA, Roosevelt's administration
had "assumed a community of interest of the managers of business corporations and the directors of government agencies."
The NIRA signaled the success of the New Deal cartelization
efforts.

Various elements in business and industry now looked forward to the NIRA's facilitation of price and production controls,
or to obtaining greater profits through emulation of their more
monopolistic colleagues, while small merchants hoped to be
saved from the onrushing chain stores and mass distributors.
Much of industry grudgingly accepted Section 7a in exchange for
exemption from the antitrust laws. Even the president of the National Association of Manufacturers, who had been hostile to

the industrial-recovery bill in its originally enacted version, now felt that industry had a right to be encouraged. "The modification of the Borah amendment," he insisted, "makes it clear that the rigid restrictions of the antitrust law are not to apply in the future." Industry would now have an opportunity to "police itself against ruthless competition in the form of unregulated price cutting."

As a result of the hopes and expectations raised by the President and Wagner among millions of exploited and suffering workers, the NIRA would insure stormy controversy and difficult days ahead. In the process of gaining support from labor and management for the NIRA, the Administration had unknowingly committed itself "to a broad policy of government intervention in collective bargaining that was to lead far beyond 7a." Most important, however, the vagueness and lack of specific direction and orientation in this enabling act would insure inevitable dissension among its administrators, conflict among groups seeking to use it for their own objectives, and a fatal inability to define and pursue a "consistent line of policy." How could it be otherwise when, for example, one clause exempted the proposed codes from the antitrust laws and another provided that no code should be so applied as "to permit monopolies or monopolistic practices, or to eliminate, oppress, or discriminate against small enterprises"?

Sidney Fine, *The Automobile Under the Blue Eagle* (Ann Arbor, Mich., 1963), 40; Bernstein, *Turbulent Years*, 34, 35, 172; *New York Times*, June 14, 17, 1933; Lyon et al., *The National Recovery Administration*, 41, 83–84, 123–24; Schlesinger, *The Coming of the New Deal*, 108–10; Hawley, *The New Deal and the Problem of Monopoly*, 33–34; Charles L. Dearing et al., *The ABC of the NRA* (Washington, D. C., 1934), 125–30; Norman Thomas, *As I See It* (New York, 1932), 38, 84; William E. Leuchtenberg, "The New Deal and the Analogue of War," in John Braeman, Robert H. Bremner, and Everett Walters, eds., *Change and Continuity in Twentieth-Century America* (Athens, Ohio, 1964), 131.

2

Power to Industry

_____

〜〜〜〜〜〜〜〜〜〜〜〜〜〜〜〜〜〜〜〜〜〜〜〜〜〜〜〜〜〜〜

AS SENATORS BORAH, LONG, and others had charged, the NIRA turned over to the President unprecedented lines of economic authority. These powers, in turn, were bequeathed to Johnson, whose initiatives, along with the decisions of the members of a business-oriented bureaucracy, were primarily responses to their own ideological background and to unremitting industry and trade-association pressures for control of production and price policies. The results were a disastrous setback for New Deal progressives, economic planners, trustbusters, social-welfare reformers, and consumer spokesmen.

From the start, the NRA became concerned with two important tasks, the making of codes and, within weeks, the formulation and acceptance of the President's Reemployment Agreement. Initially, there was an intensive effort on the part of the Recovery Administration to secure approval of codes, primarily for large industries. During the second period, emphasis shifted to the reemployment agreements, while in the third period, attention reverted to code-making and to developing machinery for code administration.

Johnson and Richberg

FDR's limited horizon was demonstrated when he viewed Title I of the NIRA as a means for long-run reform and reorganization of the economy, whereas the public-works program in Title II was, in his eyes, merely an emergency measure and not overly important. FDR further facilitated failure of the whole undertaking—if it ever had any hopes for success—when he assigned the wrong administrators to head its two independent units.

By June 1933, the nation's weakened economy required a sudden, massive infusion of jobs and increased purchasing power. This might have been achieved had Johnson, instead of Interior Secretary Harold L. Ickes, been given the reins of the public-works program under Title II. With his dynamic energies, reliance on quick, decisive action, and imaginative public appeals, Johnson would have been pouring millions of dollars into the economy within a matter of weeks, if not days. Ickes, with a keen appreciation of history, was much too distrusting and too cautious to do other than question every proposed project in the minutest detail. He feared another Teapot Dome scandal or Tammany Hall boodle if he permitted indiscriminate approval of work projects. The result was interminable delay in the start of vitally needed public works, and virtually no coordination with the NRA program under Johnson. "Honest" Harold would have been far better at the helm of the NRA, where exerting caution and taking time for the creation of a limited number of codes, and their constant subsequent appraisal, were absolutely necessary if governmental initiative and control were not to be surrendered to the trade associations in the development of industry-wide rules. The ultimate failure of the NRA was further assured by these choices in leadership.

As general counsel and second in command in the NRA, the President selected Donald R. Richberg. A man of great talent, Richberg had been reared in Victorian Chicago by a strong-willed mother—an educator turned spiritualist and practicing doctor—and by an authoritarian father who became a reform-minded leader of the local board of education. He attended the University of Chicago and Harvard Law School, and then practiced law. Frustrated by boring work, the seamy side of Chicago business and politics, and the social demands of a disappointed first wife, he found his outlet in the writing of moralistic auto-biographical novels and muckraking pieces and, finally, in involvement in reform politics.

In 1912, Richberg threw himself into the presidential campaign of the "wild, radical and dangerous" Theodore Roosevelt
of Bull Moose days. After brief employment with the Progressive
party as head of its Legislative Reference Bureau, and a period
of activity in support of American involvement in the First
World War, he became a nationally known labor advocate. As
chief counsel to the independent railroad brotherhoods and
railroad shopmen, he argued against a federal injunction with
which industry sought to destroy trade unions during the 1922
railroad shopmen's strike. In 1924, he played a leading role in
La Follette's campaign for the presidency, after which he drafted
and helped insure passage of the Labor Act of 1926, as well as
the Norris–La Guardia Anti-Injunction Act six years later. In
the 1932 presidential race, he helped write FDR's campaign
address on railroads, and served as the executive chairman of
the National Progressive League in support of Roosevelt.

When the fifty-two-year-old tall, bulky Richberg was appointed by FDR as general counsel to the NRA, progressives
and labor leaders felt assured that they could expect justice and
understanding from the New Deal. But unfortunately for trade
unions and liberals, Richberg's negative progressivisim was of
an earlier vintage, and though active in twentieth-century law
and politics, he had "remained relatively immobile in ideology."
The New Deal passed him by and gradually evolved a positive
liberalism associated with a developing welfare state, and a
degree of government involvement which went far beyond anything he and most New Nationalists had envisioned in 1912.
His values were far closer to the old liberalism of the nineteenth
century than to the belated progressivism of FDR and Harry S.
Truman.

Richberg was vulnerable to criticism, and yearned for
flattery. Thus, as general counsel of the NRA, which he soon
found to be staffed largely by representatives of management
who were hostile to his liberal reputation, Richberg bent over
backward to accommodate business and industry.

In the process of appointment as general counsel, Richberg

came away from a White House meeting with the impression that the President had assigned him the task of watchdog over Johnson, that he would hereafter enjoy a special relationship to the Chief Executive, and that authority in the NRA was to be shared between Johnson and himself. These assumptions would eventually lead to a serious clash between these two sensitive spokesmen.

Defying general expectations, Richberg assumed what he deemed to be an impartial stance as an arbiter among business, labor, and government, instead of acting as an outspoken protector of labor. Accordingly, he raised no objections to Johnson's appointment of top-management bureaucracy to key NRA positions, which not only insured dominance by business interests but underscored Johnson's bias against organized labor and the consumer. Instead of providing for business, government, and labor cooperation, the new bureaucrats undermined the role of the NRA as a guardian against abuses of the privileges accorded business by suspension of the antitrust laws.

Richberg soon relinquished active management of a sprawling Legal Division to his assistant general counsel. Thereafter, he devoted major attention to working closely with Johnson, mediated special problems and industrial disputes, advised the President on internal NRA policy decisions and on manifestations of cooperation or resistance in industry, and spoke nationwide in behalf of the NRA.

Vadney, *The Wayward Liberal,* 3–14, Chs. II–IV; Richberg, *The Rainbow,* 111–12; Richberg, *My Hero: The Indiscreet Memoirs of an Eventful but Unheroic Life* (New York, 1954), 162–63, 165–66, 168–69; Hawley, *The New Deal and the Problem of Monopoly,* 56–57; Johnson, *The Blue Eagle,* 206, 212–19.

The General Commands a Bureaucracy

And what of Johnson? Was he to be supreme, or one among equals? Not only did he have to contend with Richberg, who felt free to report directly to FDR, but he also had to cope with the

Special Industrial Recovery Board, and subsequently with other administrative units.

The Special Industrial Recovery Board was created by the President to provide overall supervision of the NRA and its administrator, and was headed by Commerce Secretary Daniel C. Roper. It was composed of four Cabinet members and a number of key administrators, including the chairman of the Federal Trade Commission (FTC). It was somewhat ironic that the FTC chairman, who was the government's watchdog in the fight against monopolies and monopolistic developments, should help supervise an organization committed to circumventing the nation's antitrust laws. And when the Recovery Board did indeed demonstrate momentary independence and a penchant for criticism, Johnson established the precedent of circumventing or overwhelming the questioning group. But he really didn't have to worry, in this instance. The Cabinet members and assorted government officials were far too overwhelmed with their own burgeoning tasks to assume this additional responsibility. As one of the earliest and most perceptive students of the NRA put it, "No policies were arrived at or promulgated, and the Board was soon lost in the fast-shifting NRA scene." [1]

In an endeavor to coordinate the confusing and conflicting administrative bureaucracies which continued to blossom under the early New Deal, the President organized an Executive Council in July 1933. This was an enlarged cabinet with Frank Walker, Roosevelt's devoted friend, as executive secretary. When he found the Executive Council too cumbersome for discussion and decision-making, Roosevelt created the National Emergency Council (NEC), on November 17, 1933.[2] The NEC was warmly welcomed, for a time, as the planning agency that

1. Lyon et al., *The National Recovery Administration,* 44.
2. The National Emergency Council was to be composed of the following, and such other members as the President might designate: Secretaries of Interior, Agriculture, Commerce, and Labor, the administrators of Agriculture Adjustment and Federal Emergency Relief, the chairman of the Home Owners Loan Corporation, the Governor of the Farm Credit Administration, and a representative of the Consumers' Council.

would clear away the confusion and competition of administrative agencies in decision-making.

Roosevelt sought to transfer the functions of the Special Industrial Recovery Board to the National Emergency Council, now the projected policy coordinator for the NRA. But this move too failed, because the exact relationship between the National Emergency Council and the NRA was never clearly defined. Furthermore, there was no evidence that it functioned any more effectively as a general control agency for the NRA than did the Special Industrial Recovery Board. The failure of the Special Industrial Recovery Board, and its successors, effectively to stabilize and coordinate NRA policies and methods made it certain, unfortunately, that Johnson would be free of control by any supervisory or policy-making board. And the President was far too busy, and ineffective as an administrator, to pull in the reins on the general, until it was too late.

By means of executive orders issued through December 1933, the President delegated many of his powers to Johnson, enabling the latter to appoint personnel, fix their compensation, conduct hearings, approve codes except for major industries, and affirm changes in codes—all seemingly subject to the general approval of the Special Industrial Recovery Board.

In less than two years, the NRA developed into a sprawling administrative colossus, dealing with the employers of 22 million pre-depression workers, and establishing controls over production and prices which affected every consumer in the nation. Before it went out of existence, the NRA negotiated and approved 546 codes of fair competition and 185 supplemental codes, filling eighteen volumes and thirteen thousand pages; released some eleven thousand administrative orders interpreting the codes; and influenced the President to issue seventy executive orders dealing with rights, procedure, and privileges under the NRA. Most of these orders and rulings had the full force and effect of law.

The staff of the NRA ranged from about 400 in August 1933, when its monthly expenditure was $393,000, to a high of

4,500 in February 1935, when it disbursed $1,054,000 for the month. The NRA became a unique New Deal agency, for it interpreted a legislative act—the NIRA—and to a limited extent, adjudicated its own administrative decisions. In fact, the NRA became so broad in its powers that eventually it was legislating by decree. Public policy was determined by an administrative bureaucracy whose members were as politically partisan as the members of Congress, yet at times assumed far greater power than that constitutionally assigned the lawmakers.

Lyon et al., *The National Recovery Administration,* 29–31, 43, 44; Exec. Order No. 6205-A, July 15, 1933; Exec. Order No. 6543-A, December 30, 1933.

The Code-Making Process

Within days after passage of the NIRA, Johnson was entreating, cajoling, and threatening the large industrial groups to hasten the submission of proposed codes of fair competition. He insisted that the success or failure of this great venture would be determined in little more than two months, and sought quick agreement on maximum hours of work, minimum wage rates, and industrial self-government and cooperation. The Act furnished few specific weapons beyond licensing, but he seemed determined, at first, to curb price raising and profit taking. However, in this as in other matters, competing group pressures, as well as Johnson's personality, haste, and contradictory decisions, helped doom the venture. Apparently convinced that the Act was unconstitutional, and could not be sustained by the courts, he refused to invoke any of its licensing powers. And without this weapon, he was unable to enforce the code provisions against recalcitrant employers or violators. Thus, the major "weapons" left him were moral suasion and public pressure, those which he had used some sixteen years earlier to whip up war patriotism. Furthermore, in the process of facilitating speedy codification, he made extreme, damaging concessions to industry, many of which retarded the nation's recovery in 1933.

After six weeks of wrangling with spokesmen from key industries, Johnson was able to look back upon only one major breakthrough—the cotton-textile code. But this was not necessarily the result of his personal influence, for the cotton trade association had long sought industry-wide agreements and had been prepared with a draft code the day the NIRA was adopted.

The rules, regulations, and administrative procedures to facilitate the formulation of codes of fair competition were prescribed by executive order or determined by Johnson's decisions. To its organization of officials and its legal and research divisions, the NRA added three advisory boards, to represent business, labor, and the consumer.

Although there was no uniformity among the codes, or in the time consumed from initial preparation to final approval, or in the problems confronted during any stage in the code-making process, the plan for code-making generally adhered to the following steps: The applicant, representing a trade or industry-wide group, submitted a tentative code which was assigned to a deputy administrator. When the group had been affirmed as properly representative, preliminary conferences were held, supervised by the deputy administrator. Those attending included the code committee of the applicant group, and a representative from each of the three advisory boards, from the Legal Division, and from the Research and Planning Division. When the deputy felt that the conferees had reached a consensus, and that the proposals were in suitable form, a public hearing was convened at which interested parties could testify. After the consideration of any new viewpoints or amendments suggested at the hearings, the proposals were submitted to another stage of negotiations, from which evolved the document which the deputy sent on to the NRA administrator.

After Johnson considered the possible impact of the proposed code upon the nation's economy, and its relationship to the public interest, the final step was to advise the President as to whether it should be approved, modified, or rejected.

Those having greatest impact in the formulation of these

codes were the deputy administrators, who, like most members of the War Industries Board of the First World War, had been drawn from the ranks of business. Johnson's key subordinates— Alvin Brown, Robert W. Lea, Kenneth Simpson, Arthur D. Whiteside, Clarence Williams, and Malcolm Muir—had industrial and military backgrounds and shared the judgments and sympathies of business. They were not prepared to police management rigorously and, like Johnson, hesitated to insert in the codes any items which businessmen firmly disliked. Not only did the General and his key staff avoid possible prosecution of NRA violators, but when Henry Ford refused to sign the automobile code later in the year, Johnson and the NRA retreated, and they became increasingly mild in the face of challenges from other facets of industry.

New York Times, June 21, 22, 1933; Lyon et al., *The National Recovery Administration*, 84; Louis Galambos, *Competition and Cooperation: The Emergence of a National Trade Association* (Baltimore, 1966), 173–202.

The Advisory Boards

On the naïve theory that the Recovery Administration was an impartial umpire, not to control or be controlled by its advisers, the appointment of the twenty-one members of the Industrial Advisory Board was made by the Secretary of Commerce. The recommendations of these business leaders were advisory to Hugh Johnson and his staff. In code negotiations, this board was represented by a staff of advisers who were either permanent or loaned by business concerns. As events developed, the industrial advisers gave active support to the trade or industry-wide applicants in the bargaining process with labor representatives, and basically ignored the consumer representatives, who lacked organized group support.

The members of the Labor Advisory Board (LAB) were appointed by the Secretary of Labor, and consisted of labor leaders, one or two public-spirited citizens who could presumably speak for unorganized workers, and a permanent staff of labor specialists. This board established such goals for labor bargaining as adequate labor representation in code administration, restriction of homework, and safety and health provisions. Its executive director supervised the activities of the labor advisers in the code-making process. The Labor Board functioned as a comparatively well-defined and relatively well-implemented element in code bargaining. As the chief antagonist of the trade or industry-wide applicant, it always pressed for concessions favorable to workers. The limited degree of success attained by the Labor Board in code negotiations was determined by certain advantages given it by Section 7a of the NIRA, the competency of the labor advisers in the bargaining procedure, and the strength of organized labor in the industry or trade involved. More often than not, employers were in a strategic position to resist labor demands because the trade union in their particular industry was weak, in a state of infancy, or nonexistent. Furthermore, the staff, resources, and research skills of management were far more adequate and more highly developed than those of the insecure, fledgling trade-union movement. This was made clear when code after code was written by technicians from business and industry, on temporary loan to government.

The Consumers' Advisory Board (CAB) was unique among the advisory groups. Established to protect the interest of the consumer, it existed at the behest, and under the control, of Johnson, not of one of the independent Cabinet departments. Symbolic of Johnson's attitude toward this board was the fact that not until precedent-forming codes had been adopted, around mid-September, did he require that the deputy administrator's report recommending approval of a code be accompanied by a written opinion from the Consumers' Advisory Board. But most meaningful was the realization that this board lacked the support of any well-organized or articulate constituency. Without the backing of an effective pressure group or a Ralph Nader, it was sidetracked in the negotiating process, and unable to carry out its mandate to appraise every agreement and hearing to see that nothing was done to the detriment of the consumer community.

This situation enabled Johnson to establish a pattern which, with rare exceptions, was adhered to by the NRA staff—that of ignoring the questioning and challenging of Consumers' Advisory Board representatives.[3] In the process, Johnson abandoned a major task of the Administration: to be "directly responsible for safe-guarding the public welfare."

Lyon et al., *The National Recovery Administration*, 120–23, 123–29.

The Textile Code: A Precedent

As his hastily assembled staff prepared for the public-hearing phase of the formulation of the proposed textile code, during the last days of June, the General displayed a disturbing facet of his character and leadership. He suddenly, and unexpectedly, altered his position on a vital issue. Uncertain of himself, Johnson easily succumbed to unyielding pressures from industry. Johnson had originally been opposed to all elements of price-fixing, while his business-oriented staff strongly recommended its adoption as compensation to industry for the costs of increased employment and wages. On June 23, the General sent out shock waves when he reversed himself and permitted the

3. The Consumers' Advisory Board, appointed on June 26, 1933, was chaired by Mary Harriman Rumsey, and also included President Frank P. Graham of the University of North Carolina; economics professor William F. Ogburn of the University of Chicago; President Belle Sherwin of the National League of Women Voters; Mrs. Joseph Daniels of the Indiana League of Women Voters; Professor Alonzo E. Taylor, director of the Food Research Institute at Stanford University; and Lucius R. Eastman, president of the American Arbitration Association. Among other members at various times were economist Paul H. Douglas of the University of Chicago; sociologist Robert S. Lynd, coauthor of the Middletown series; economist William T. Foster; George Stocking of the University of Texas; Walton H. Hamilton of Yale Law School; Stacy May, an economist for the Rockefeller Foundation; Frederic C. Howe, a former muckraker, now of the Consumers' Council for the AAA; Gardiner Means and Louis H. Bean, economists for the Department of Agriculture; and Thomas Blaisdell, professor of economics at Columbia University.

fixing of prices. This insured, as a start, that the enterprises in an industry could agree among themselves not to sell under the cost of production, whatever that meant. To progressives, this change of heart was additional evidence of Johnson's bias toward business. The White House went along with the General's new approach.

Meanwhile, on another front, organized labor was quick to resort to the Labor Advisory Board when it learned of the General's tentative decision to exclude guarantees of collective bargaining from the fair-competition codes under negotiation. Within little more than a week after enactment of the bill, the future of the recovery plan was at stake. Workers throughout the country suddenly found themselves on the defensive, forced to battle for collective-bargaining rights theoretically assured them by the NRA. Reports of management coercion and domination through hastily organized company unions, particularly in steel and coal, flowed into Washington. These led Labor Secretary Perkins, who also headed the Labor Advisory Board,[4] to charge that company unions were not representative of the collective will of the workers. Partly in reaction to Johnson's and Richberg's increasing support of industry in the writing and enforcing of codes, the Labor Advisory Board sought to reshape itself as a forceful adviser and as labor's active pressure group in the formulation of the cotton-textile code and subsequent agreements.

The cotton-textile industry was a major one; its mills sprawled from Maine to Alabama and it employed, during the depths of the depression in March 1933, 314,000 workers—more than steel. Suffering throughout the prosperous 1920s from overcapacity, the industry approached catastrophe after 1929 because of excess output, price-cutting, low profits which

---

4. The Labor Advisory Board was composed of William Green, John L. Lewis, John P. Frey, head of the Metal Trade Department of the AF of L, Rose Schneiderman, president of the Women's Trade Union League, Sidney Hillman, president of the Amalgamated Clothing Workers, and Rev. Francis J. Haas of the National Catholic Welfare Conference.

became losses, and increasingly inhumane working conditions. Although the number of spindles decreased significantly during the eight years prior to 1933, production increased as a result of night work. Between 1929 and 1933, employment dropped by 26 percent, excluding part-time workers. Wages fell to five dollars a week for many, in payment for fifty to fifty-five hours of work.

Cold statistics, however, could not convey a picture of the rampant fear and misery which engulfed textile communities, particularly in the South. Quoting from reports to Harry Hopkins, labor historian Irving Bernstein has drawn a devastating picture of the times. Textile workers lived in "feverish terror" of mill closings, of part-time wages below the level needed to buy food, of physical and mental exhaustion caused by the "stretch-out" (increased machine loads), of discharge for union activity, and of keeping children out of school for lack of adequate clothes or shoes. Medical care was rare, and syphilis was uncured and unchecked. Malnutrition and dietary diseases were extensive, while fatigue lined the faces of men and women workers. Their housing was often insufferably inadequate, to be compared unfavorably with the worst of European hovels.

The situation was not much better in New England. Many companies closed their New England mills and fled to the lower-paying South. Unemployment drove the jobless into "a state of semi-collapse; cracking nerves; and an overpowering terror of the future." Even the young had become apathetic and despairing.[5]

Testifying at the cotton-textile hearings which began on June 27, 1933, in the new Commerce Building, George A. Sloan voiced the hopes of industry's Cotton-Textile Institute, which he headed. He welcomed the NRA as an endeavor to cope with industrial overcapacity and outlined a code which would reduce the average work week from fifty hours to forty, and increase the wage scale to a weekly minimum of eleven dollars in the North and ten dollars in the South. Before the week was out,

5. Bernstein, *Turbulent Years,* 299–300.

however, Sloan reluctantly responded to harsh criticism from progressive congressmen and William Green, by agreeing to the abolition of child labor, below the age of sixteen, and the increase of minimum wages by another two dollars.

In the publicity and excitement which followed ratification of this first code, which had been fashioned in just a month, most Americans were mistakenly convinced that they had witnessed a rare spectacle, if not a social and economic millennium. Acting in a manner in evident contrast to that of the destructive industrial leadership which had often plagued the 1920s, industrial management had sat down with labor and apparently agreed upon the acceptance of Section 7a, the abolition of child labor, greatly reduced maximum hours, and significantly increased minimum wages.

Signed by the President on July 9, 1933, this code of fair competition included provisions which management would subsequently pervert in order to circumvent the humane objectives of the NIRA; these clauses exempted cleaners, outside employees, and "learners" from the wage minimum. The pleas of Senator Black and William Green for a thirty-hour work week to insure significant reemployment were overlooked. The warning of Sidney Hillman, head of the Amalgamated Clothing Workers, that there would be little substantial reemployment in the clothing industry with acceptance of a forty-hour work week was ignored. The extremely low level of the minimum wage, which made it simple for employers to dispense with child labor, was forgotten. And in the initial, enthusiastic response to this first NRA achievement, the implications surrounding creation of the Cotton Textile Industry Committee were shunted aside. Headed by Sloan, this new committee consisted of his institute and of representatives of other trade associations; it was to officially administer the cotton-textile code. A pattern was set for other industries: management spokesmen would repeatedly be sustained by the federal government in formulating, interpreting, and administering codes of fair competition.

Each textile mill was to have an industrial relations committee with employer and employee representation, to which controversies would be referred. Unsettled disputes went to a state Industrial Relations Board and then, if necessary, to a tripartite Cotton Textile National Industrial Relations Board. The exploited, fearful textile worker never received any justice from the Textile Board because its chairman, economist Robert W. Bruere, was too weak to face up to industry's wrongdoings. The labor representative, President George L. Berry of the Printing Pressmen, never took his job seriously, and the industry designee, President B. E. Greer of Furman University, was an ardent advocate for Southern textile interests. The individual who ran the Textile Board was Sloan, who made certain that industry never policed itself for the benefit of workers or consumers.

Of crucial significance, furthermore, was a clause which labor and civic spokesmen had neglected to challenge, one which not only established a precedent for other industries but exacerbated some of the key contradictions in the New Deal recovery plan. This provided that production machinery in the cotton-textile industry would not be permitted to operate for more than two shifts of a forty-hour work week. This requirement forced some companies to lay off workers immediately, including a third of the employees of a large textile concern, and the overall principle established for the nation was one of planned production limitation, alongside price-fixing. At one of the most critical moments in the nation's history, when a great need was to increase the purchasing power of the consumer through immediate expansion in production, jobs, and income, the NRA established a restrictionist policy. The precedent was self-defeating, for almost every other industry insisted on similar rights.

New York Times, June 21–28, 1933; Bernstein, *Turbulent Years,* 299–300, 302–4; NRA, Transcript of Hearing No. 1, June 27–30, 1933, in RG 9, 7152, National Archives; Galambos, *Competition and Cooperation,* 203–26, 230–31.

Industry Dominates the Codes

How was it possible for the New Deal to sanction such extreme concessions to industry?

At the time the cotton-textile code was formulated, the United Textile Workers of America (UTWA) was one of the weak unions which leaned heavily upon the NRA. The UTWA membership included, at first, less than 5 percent of the employed workers, with virtually none in the South, where the industry was concentrated. Furthermore, it was led by Thomas F. McMahon, an incompetent trade unionist who had never recovered from the fearful setbacks of the 1920s. As a result, the UTWA had no leverage with which to exert influence upon Roosevelt and an industry-oriented NRA deputy administrator and staff.

When the Administration selected the self-government pattern of regulation, a dominant place was automatically assured trade associations, for they were the best-organized forces available. As a result, not only did officials of existing associations actively initiate a majority of the codes, but the code system became largely a direct offshoot of the trade-association system.

While experts and lobbyists represented trade associations with economic and political prowess, there were no well-prepared labor and consumer bureaucrats appointed to key NRA posts to counter the potency of business power. And men like Paul H. Douglas of the University of Chicago, Leon Henderson of the Russell Sage Foundation, sociologist Robert S. Lynd, former muckraker Frederic C. Howe, President Frank P. Graham of the University of North Carolina, and economists Gardiner Means and Thomas Blaisdell were available for such appointments. The rare independent government spokesman was untrained, and wilted under the pressure of Johnson's inhuman work schedule. Believing that the NRA was an end in itself, that codification of every industry, large and small, would insure a dramatic upturn in the economy, if not its recovery, Johnson was willing to offer endless concessions to industry in order to secure speedy agreement on codes.

Between June and October 1933, at least six hundred proposed codes received varying degrees of superficial scrutiny from
a harassed, inadequately staffed Code Analysis Division which
lacked basic data. This division determined whether the applicant group was representative of its industry or trade, and
evaluated the economic and social significance of specific code
proposals. Because of Johnson's unyielding pressure, many
codes were never scrutinized by the Code Analysis Division.
After a while, proposed codes were simply assigned to the
next available deputy administrator, irrespective of interest,
background, or ability.

As a result of the demand for speed, deputy administrators
tended to become active, instead of covert, proponents for management. And the highly efficient Industrial Advisory Board
easily countered the efforts of the Labor and Consumers' Boards.
In the process, control and administration of the codes slipped
out of the hands of government officials and into those of management representatives.

Seeking to play a role in the formulation of the codes, the
Consumers' Advisory Board tried unsuccessfully to become the
active protector of the "public interest." The response of an
irritated, intolerant Johnson was to isolate and then negate the
work of the one board whose interests extended beyond those
of labor or industry alone. In an attempt to adopt practices
which should have been followed by the entire NRA staff, the
Consumers' Advisory Board sought the compilation of basic
economic data, and the analysis and evaluation of specific proposals in terms of their overall impact. This time-consuming
process was a direct challenge to the haste, the procedures, and
the precedents established under Johnson. More or less representative of his approach was the week in which the Board was
requested to react officially to the provisions of seventy-three
codes, covering a wide variety of industries.

The consumer representative, then, was either overwhelmed,
circumvented, or ignored in the negotiating process. On most
occasions, Board members were obliged to go over the heads

of Johnson and Richberg and appeal directly to sympathetic lawmakers and to the press. In the absence of any strong consumer or third-party movement, and with organized labor surrendering responsible control over code authorities, it was inevitable that restrictionism and price-fixing would become the prevailing pattern.

The NRA staff was unprepared either to classify industries uniformly prior to the negotiation of labor and trade provisions, or to provide for subsequent administration of the codes. The result was chaos: major codes were approved which cut segments out of other industries and trades, and time and energy were squandered on insignificant codes which had no business being adopted in the early stages of the NRA.

Finally, the manner in which code authorities were created to administer and enforce the codes was another illustration of how businessmen gained sweeping governmental powers, and refused to share them with labor and consumer representatives. Most code authorities were given extensive power to interpret codes, grant exemptions, and exercise quasi-legislative and quasi-judicial functions, without any real governmental supervision. Provisions for maximum prices, salary limitations, and profit controls were nonexistent. Having been selected by trade associations, or in association-dominated elections, code-authority members were almost exclusively businessmen. Less than 10 percent of the code authorities had some labor representation, and little more than 1 percent had consumer spokesmen. The government members were themselves usually businessmen, who helped facilitate control by trade associations and, therefore, the evolution of industrial self-government.

Unlimited relief was accorded most large businessmen from the start. Emulating the textile code, sixty-one subsequent codes set limitations on machine or plant hours. Over thirty industries won approval for restrictions on producing capacity through limiting new construction and preventing the opening of closed plants.

The second code adopted prohibited selling below "cost,"

by which industry really meant the price then prevailing. This proviso eventually appeared in some four hundred codes.

In the first twenty codes, Johnson and his deputies established precedents for almost every conceivable kind of quasi-monopolistic practice injurious to the consumer. They facilitated the adoption, as well as the acceptance as a public service, of activities which had once been defined as "conspiracy, in restraint of trade." While the deputy administrators and Johnson bowed to the demands of industry, the hopes and expectations of organized labor and the consumer were circumscribed or suppressed.

Hawley, *The New Deal and the Problem of Monopoly,* 56, 57–62; Lyon et al., *The National Recovery Administration,* 93, 120–23, 129–31, 136–37, 166, 212, 224, 267, 275, 280, 427–44, 566–77, 585–89, 599–601, 610–11, 623–37, 653–69, 689–94, 706; Schlesinger, *The Coming of the New Deal,* 125–26; Saul Nelson, *NRA Work Materials 56, Minimum Price Regulation Under Codes of Fair Competition* (Washington, D. C., 1936), 23–24; Charles F. Roos, *NRA Economic Planning* (Bloomington, Ind., 1937), 249–50, 277–79; Enid Baird, *NRA Work Materials 76, Price Filing Under NRA Codes* (Washington, D. C., 1936), 21, 445–47; Richberg, *The Rainbow,* 120–24; *NRA Work Materials 46, Code Authorities and Their Part in the Administration of NIRA* (Washington, D. C., 1936), 69, 120, 132–37, 161–63.

The President's Reemployment Agreement

By July 9, 1933, when the President approved the final draft of the cotton-textile agreement, not one other major industry had submitted, or been willing to submit, an acceptable code to be used as a basis for public discussion. The hostile National Association of Manufacturers, and key business leaders, tended to drag their feet because they feared the impact of significantly reduced work weeks, or of what they deemed enforced unionization. Meanwhile, the Public Works Administration, under Ickes, was trickling money into the nation's coffers at such a slow pace that it provided no significant uplift to the economy.

With failure staring him in the face and without an effective weapon with which to force compliance, the General sought to whip up public enthusiasm and catalyze American industry into subscribing to NRA codes. Finally, Johnson the magician brought forth what seemed to be a simple, appealing document, the so-called "blanket code." To afford more time for the drafting and acceptance of their special codes, American industry and business were asked to endorse a simple pledge to uphold, in the interim, NRA standards with respect to minimum wages, maximum hours of work, and the rights of labor (Section 7a). In spite of the initial opposition of Cabinet members in the Special Industrial Recovery Board, who feared that resort to the emotionalism and pageantry which Johnson projected might revive the hysteria and intolerance which had scarred this nation during the First World War, the General finally convinced the President and a Cabinet majority to endorse this blanket agreement. Along with it went a campaign of patriotic fervor unmatched since the days of the War Industries Board.

On July 19, the day that Johnson secured the Chief Executive's endorsement of the blanket code—to be known as the President's Reemployment Agreement (PRA)—a frightening shudder went through the nation's economy when prices on the New York Stock Exchange dropped precipitously. It should have been clear to perceptive observers that the dramatic increase in production, and to a lesser extent in employment, since March, which the Administration, industry, and organized labor had been hailing as the start of a steady return to prosperity, was merely a temporary and unsubstantial development. Industrial and retail interests had increased their manufacturing and purchasing as they anticipated higher costs under NRA codification; others had reacted to a purely speculative fever in hopes of benefiting from projected monetary inflation. Shortly thereafter, FDR attempted to brush aside the new business slump as normal, and the ensuing drop in production and stock prices as merely corrective.

The day after the dramatic stock-market collapse, FDR

began to lay the basis for support of the voluntary blanket compact establishing a thirty-five-hour industrial week at a forty-cent-per-hour minimum, and a forty-hour week for white-collar workers, with a twelve-to-fifteen-dollar weekly minimum. In a nationwide radio address, he appealed for unified action to spur recovery and asked the country's five million employers to wire acceptance of his Reemployment Agreement. As a stimulant, he reminded them of the "economic hell" of the last few years, caused by a few selfish men. Within an hour, more than five thousand telegrams of support from all walks of life poured into Washington, and a steady stream of endorsements continued through the next few days.

On August 1, Johnson officially opened a thirty-day drive for the President's Reemployment Agreement, adopting as the campaign insignia the Navajo thunderbird, or Blue Eagle. This symbol of a nonindustrial civilization was poised above the legend "We Do Our Part," with "NRA" inscribed overhead. Seeking to enlist industry adherence through December 31, pending approval of codes of fair competition, the Blue Eagle drive transplanted the insignia to millions of posters, billboards, flags, and movie screens, which looked down upon the citizenry from every angle and vantage point. The emotional rhetoric and hysterical appeals of the First World War were taken from the shelves, dusted off, and brought up to date.

Charles S. Horner, who had directed the Liberty Loan drives of the First World War, helped organize the campaign, and Johnson and thousands of four-minute speakers flooded the nation with propaganda from the radio, pulpits, and lecterns. The country was asked to join the war against the depression, against "industrial pirates," against "cutthroat and monopolistic price slashing," and against "chiselers." Even the President joined in the public-relations planning when he asked the General if it would not be wise to get "a list of the big companies who will sign . . . the voluntary agreements and release it for Wednesday morning papers and follow each day with a number of big companies? I think the little fellows will follow the leader." [6]

The Blue Eagle symbol of faith soon reigned supreme over mass meetings and gigantic parades in communities large and small, coupled with blaring bands seeking to reassure a befogged public, as in a holy crusade, that "Happy Days Are Here Again." The Blue Eagle parade in New York was the largest in that city's history, as a quarter of a million people marched up Fifth Avenue through the afternoon and on into the night, while millions cheered from the sidewalks. Johnson used the rallies, parades, and four-minute speakers to whip up public enthusiasm and convince millions of employers to sign the NRA pledges, in the expectation that this would automatically insure rising wages and millions of new jobs by Labor Day. Carried away by his own enthusiasm, he predicted that the blanket agreement would insure the rehiring of five to six million workers in little more than a month. The next day he ventured a more conservative estimate—that three million would be reemployed within a two-month period. How different were these predictions from Herbert Hoover's appeals, during his administration, to retain faith in the nation, in the expectation that prosperity was "just around the corner"? Unfortunately, attention to the rest of the New Deal's recovery program was all but shunted aside as increasing numbers of Americans looked to the flamboyant General to save the nation.

The Blue Eagle drive did help speed up submission and approval of many code proposals. Noting that the earliest code-seeking groups were being granted various inducements to sign a code, such as price-control devices and other powers to regulate trade practices, many employers decided it was more beneficial to subscribe to a code, rather than merely the President's Reemployment Agreement, which gave them the psychological satisfaction of participating in a patriotic campaign but no assurance of material benefits. The overall result was an

6. FDR to Johnson, July 25, 1933, Roosevelt Papers, OF 466.

acceleration of the codification of American industry, to the general detriment of the consumer.

NRA News Release No. 33, July 7, 1933; *New York Times,* July 20–23, 25–29, 1933; Lyon et al., *The National Recovery Administration,* 94; Johnson, *The Blue Eagle,* 169, 177, 262.

The Final Codes

By the time public hearings on the steel code commenced in early August, the offices of the NRA in the immense Commerce Building in Washington (Herbert Hoover's pride and joy, with some ten thousand offices and no parking space) were a madhouse. Telephone service had all but broken down, with an estimated six hundred long-distance callers an hour asking questions, pledging or rejecting cooperation. Long lines of individuals in the Information Room waited to make inquiries, while in the Press Room tables were piled high with news releases and telephones for bustling newsmen.

The big, oblong theater of the building overflowed with coatless, perspiring men and women gazing straight ahead at the stage, where sat the NRA advisory boards. Johnson was in the chair during the early hearings. Tall, thin, balding Robert P. Lamont, secretary of commerce under Hoover, but now president of the employers' Iron and Steel Institute, spoke for a segment of American industry which still worked thousands of employees twelve hours daily, and on occasion seven days per week. Mumbling his testimony in a monotone, Lamont underscored the generosity of steel owners to workers, and contended that the industry would go bankrupt if it had to increase wages any more. Finally, he insisted that workers were more than satisfied with existing company unions. After Johnson rejected Lamont's defense of compulsory company unions, and the steel owners called a recess of ten minutes, Lamont unenthusiastically endorsed the basic statements of the Recovery Act.

Frances Perkins, who had just returned from meetings with

steel workers in Pennsylvania and West Virginia, was appalled by the prevalence of the twelve-hour day and seven-day week. She insisted that the wages offered by the steel companies did not provide workers with a decent standard of living, and urged, in addition, effective guarantees against child labor, and legislation providing for unemployment insurance. Less than two months after the enactment of the NIRA, the Secretary of Labor was alert to the tendency of some industrialists to sabotage the government's program, to refuse to write codes, or as a last resort, to write impossibly bad ones. Many of them, in fact, were participating in the "strike of the folded arms" and awaited the ending of the Great Depression by the "natural process."

The steel code, as eventually approved by the President toward the end of August for a ninety-day trial period, recognized the right of workers to collective bargaining and eliminated the open-shop clause. But its wage and hour provisions were substantially those proposed by the steel operators, which Secretary Perkins had denounced as totally inadequate to bring about any real measure of recovery in the industry. This code also included a number of provisions which enabled industry leaders to circumvent the antitrust laws legally.

Success finally seemed to have crowned the exhausting efforts of Johnson and the Recovery Administration in late August when the President approved codes not only for the steel industry but for the petroleum, lumber, and automobile industries as well. The bituminous coal code, adopted on September 18, demonstrated the determination and effectiveness of John L. Lewis' dramatic organizing drive among miners, for the coal operators agreed, in essence, to recognize the United Mine Workers as the sole union for all of their workers. With the approval of the coal code virtually all the major industries had been codified. The NRA staff struggled for months thereafter with hundreds of codes for minor industries, but the pattern had been set.

In the midst of signing the first wave of major codes, an

overly optimistic President informed an enthusiastic audience
of five thousand who had gathered on the beautiful campus of
Vassar College, near his Hyde Park home, that the nation had
started on an upward surge. The country was returning to "better
times," inspired by a unity unmatched since 1917. All this he
ascribed to the recently approved NRA codes which, he felt,
guaranteed that the few would no longer exploit the many.

   Despite this flood tide of codification, internal crises built
up in the NRA. They might have been eased, somewhat, by a
vastly expanded public-works program to help restore consumer
purchasing power. But it was apparent to a number of perceptive
Washington observers, and to outspoken progressives, that the
industrial aspect of FDR's recovery program was faltering
badly. It was not insuring a generally revived economy, and
could not hope to do so unless the NRA's policies were drastically altered and Johnson's leadership severely curtailed.

   Bruce Bliven in *New Republic,* August 16, 1933, 9–11; *New
York Times,* August 27, 1933.

3

The Impact Is Negative

∿∿∿∿∿∿∿∿∿∿∿∿∿∿∿∿∿∿∿∿∿∿∿∿∿∿∿∿∿∿∿∿∿∿∿∿∿

LONG BEFORE THE END of the 1933 summer, progressives were loudly lamenting the role of contemporary "robber barons," the sharp rise in prices and production, but not wages, and the humiliating spectacle of a government afraid to enforce NRA rules and regulations. Some underscored the embattled opposition of "Tory capitalists," in textile, steel, auto, and other industries, whose hands were already "stained with the blood" of the debilitated workers they had exploited regardless of the cost in human misery.

Within weeks of adoption of the textile code, hundreds of complaints started streaming in from the South. Some mill owners were discharging old employees and rehiring them as "learners," who could be paid less than the minimum for a number of weeks. Others expanded the use of the stretch-out system, whereby workers were required to handle many more looms than previously. And still other managers failed to pay overtime to maintenance employees, and resorted to general discrimination against minority and union workers. By the latter part of August, William Green was advised by his personal representative in the South: "No mills that I know of are living up to the code as signed by the President." Absolutely nothing was ever done about these destructive evasions by Sloan's textile-code authority, though Johnson would hysterically denounce these mill owners as "chiselers." That was about as far as the General went.

T.R.B. in *New Republic,* August 16, 1933, 19–20; *New Republic,* August 30, 1933, 75–76

Labor and the Consumer Suffer

Despite the NRA, the tendency of many employers to use force and repression against employees was on the increase everywhere, along with extensive violations of civil liberties that were brought to the attention of the President. Thousands of workers, seeking to organize and secure vital improvements, were meeting the same kind of oppression that had plagued the nation during the 1920s—discrimination, injunctions, martial law, and shootings by company gunmen. Within eight months of FDR's inaugural nearly two hundred workers had been shot down and at least fifteen killed by police, company guards, or vigilantes. Scores had been terrorized, tear-gassed or beaten with riot sticks. In Corinth, Mississippi, three organizers for the Amalgamated Clothing Workers were accosted on the street, kidnapped, and then escorted to the Tennessee line by men in two automobiles. Nearly three hundred strikes erupted in July alone, with four hundred reported in August, compared with some forty in the same months the previous year. Workdays lost, under 603,000 monthly in the first half of 1933, spurted to 1,375,000 in July alone, and to 2,378,000 in August. During 1933, primarily after enactment of the NIRA, there occurred the largest number of work stoppages since 1921. The overriding issue in these disputes was the right to bargain collectively.

In the meantime, the real gain in purchasing power which farmers and employed workers enjoyed between February and June 1933 was significantly reduced in July and August by a rapid rise in retail prices. This reversal in trend, according to a survey for the National Bureau of Economic Research, was accompanied by a decline in the actual per capita earnings of employed manufacturing labor.

Data issued by the Bureau of Labor Statistics on the effects of the codes, in the period between July 15 and August 15, in woolen and worsted goods, electrical machinery, dyeing and finishing, shipbuilding, and cotton goods, suggested that, except in the cotton-textile industry, the purchasing power of individual workers had not increased. Although wage rates tended to rise as work hours fell, the average weekly pay increased minutely in one of these industries, dropped in three others, and rose significantly only in cotton goods—from $11.36 to $13.17, for a 36.5-hour work week.

The forty-hour work week, which had been written into the great majority of codes and agreements, had very little effect in bringing about speedy reabsorption of the idle. Because of a general increase in the productive capacity of individual workers since 1929, those already working during the summer of 1933 could, in nearly every field, readily absorb a considerably increased volume of business before additional help was needed. Furthermore, although the government claimed that some two million workers had gained employment through NRA efforts in July and August, approximately eleven million remained unemployed.

These saddening developments moved one liberal weekly to lament that "the country will not long contemplate such a spectacle, and the sooner the President and his Recovery Administration realize this, the better."

By September, waves of discouragement began to flow across the country, especially affecting those who had placed much of their faith in Johnson's propaganda. The speculative boom had collapsed on July 19 with a roar, and economic indices began falling. Increasing numbers came to accept the warnings of progressives, and the Consumers' Advisory Board, that the NRA codes were the products of highly organized industry and management and fostered a policy of scarcity on the one hand and profits to new cartels on the other.

New Republic, August 23, 1933, 33, August 30, 1933, 75–76, September 13, 1933, 130–31, October 11, 1933, 242–43, December

Johnson's Leadership Falters

Farmers and workers were generally grateful for the New
Deal's energetic efforts, but they nevertheless joined the barrage of criticism leveled at Johnson and the NRA, which soon
swelled into a national roar. Elements of big business denounced
Section 7a for fostering "labor domination," "bureaucratic socialism," and red tape. Consumer and farm spokesmen complained bitterly about rising industrial prices which negated
improvements from other New Deal programs. Labor's spokesmen, seeing their organizing campaigns grind to a halt because
of NRA's refusal to cope with industry's circumvention of Section 7a through company unions, denounced the Blue Eagle as
a fraud and the advance guard of corporate fascism. William
Randolph Hearst, the outspoken publisher of a national network
of newspapers which had supported FDR in the 1932 campaign,
now spearheaded the journalistic barrage from the right. He
charged the NRA with being a "socialist dictatorship" and
demanded that the Roosevelt administration retreat from "the
theories of Karl Marx and the policies of Stalin."

The profound change in public attitude was demonstrated
by the utter failure of a highly publicized "Buy Now" campaign
which the General initiated in early October. Johnson blinded
himself to the realization that another round of keyed-up propaganda could not possibly help a New Deal recovery program
which people increasingly associated with higher prices, but
not more jobs. He soon learned that this program would fail for
the same reason that similar endeavors had suffered under
Hoover—the great majority of people just did not have the
money to spend.

Before the end of October, Johnson and the NRA bore the
brunt of complaints from many elements which had originally
pushed the NIRA: some segments of industry seeking greater

exploitation of the public were dissatisfied with code-authority interpretations which placed them at a disadvantage with rivals or suppliers; antitrusters now sheepishly admitted that the NRA was fostering monopoly; economic planners lamented that planning and controls were now in the exclusive possession of business cartels. These onrushing problems tended, at times, to overwhelm the NRA administrator. But to a large extent this situation was of his own making. He had too little facility for delegating work, and therefore tried to do too much himself. The promises he often made in the name of the NRA were much too specific and immediate. And the expectations created by the limitless propaganda which flowed from NRA headquarters were far greater than could be fulfilled. Finally, the pressure he was under, and the incapacity of some subordinates, had a recurring impact on Johnson his original enthusiasm disappeared, to be replaced by frayed nerves and a dispirited condition. When he reached such a stage, as he did within the first few months of his appointment, he sought refuge in drink, disappeared for days on end, and then suddenly returned a revived man.

Johnson and Roosevelt knew that the NRA was in deep trouble, especially in view of the expanding recession in September and October. Progressives had sought to alert the President to NRA shortcomings, and urge him to make up his mind about what he really wanted in the way of industrial democracy. His policy of consensus could not possibly placate everyone. He had to identify the opponents of his overall reform program and mobilize the support of the great numbers among the farmers, workers, and lower middle class who should have benefited most. Otherwise, the New Deal might end up being opposed by everyone. Roosevelt had to decide whether to fight or cooperate. If he accepted the advice of Mary Rumsey and her colleagues on the Consumers' Advisory Board, then he would fight. If he listened to Hugh Johnson, then the New Deal would merely "contain the old marked cards." Progressives increasingly asked the President, "Which side are you on?"

Deciding to stand by Johnson and give the NRA another chance, FDR sent Agriculture Secretary Henry A. Wallace and Hugh Johson on a good-will tour to the Midwest and the Far West, during the first week in November. The President hoped the two could quell a rising rebellion among farmers, and explain the recovery program to disenchanted workers and businessmen. As indebted farmers were still being evicted from homes, mass intimidation by neighbors remained the most effective weapon against foreclosures. And in November, Milo Reno's Farm Holiday Association was leading forceful strikes which bordered on guerilla warfare: in Iowa, one set of picket lines halted a market train and released its livestock; another burned down a railroad bridge; while a third fired into a freight train.

Wallace and Johnson were immediately greeted with a ringing manifesto, from five Midwestern governors, which indicted the NRA. This New Deal agency, they insisted, had made things much more difficult for the American farmer by causing higher prices for consumer goods at the very time that prices for farm products had dropped sharply. Wallace subsequently conceded that by November 1933 there was great indignation in farm communities for just this reason.

Instead of allaying the resentment of industrialists, small retailers, farmers, and political leaders by conciliatory and reasonable remarks, Johnson was propelled by his psychological makeup into speaking endlessly, unwisely, and belligerently. On the one hand, he lashed out at "witch-doctor critics" who threw "dead cats" at the recovery plan, while on the other, he typically invited them to join one of the NRA advisory boards. Johnson's trip with Wallace turned out to be a disaster, especially since at this time increasing thousands were in a mood of angry despair because too much had been promised too quickly. The NRA administrator convinced growing numbers of citizens that he was out to eat critics alive, and that he believed only fools and crooks could find flaws in the NRA. By the time the General returned from his tour, one newsman observed that the country was "getting bored with continued exhibitions of a fighting man 'cracking down' on everybody who gets a little out of line," except leading industrialists. Henry Wallace was far more effective because of his resort to the soft glove.

Lyon et al., *The National Recovery Administration,* 97, 100, 142–61, 489–90, 535–37, 705–9; *New York Times,* August 7, 28, October 9, 29, November 6–14, 16, 1933; Johnson, *The Blue Eagle,* 290–91; Raymond S. Rubinow, *NRA Work Materials 45-E-1, Section 7-a* (Washington, D. C., 1936), 1, 55–56, 64–66; Anna Page, *NRA Work Materials 45-B-1, Employment and Unemployment, 1929–35* (Washington, D. C., 1936), 36; George Soule in *New Republic,* October 18, 1933, 269–71; Ely C. Hutchinson, *NRA Work Materials 39, Problems of Administration in the Overlapping of Codes* (Washington, D.C., 1936), 16–30; Rexford G. Tugwell, *The Battle for Democracy* (New York, 1935), 262–63; Henry A. Wallace, *New Frontiers* (New York, 1934), 56.

Bailing Out the NRA

If Roosevelt had not come to the NRA's rescue in mid-November with a new public-works program which put millions on the federal payroll before Christmas, cyncism and despair might have run rampant throughout the country. Within a fortnight of its creation as a counterbalance to Ickes' turtle-like PWA, the Civil Works Administration (CWA), under Harry Hopkins, was distributing paychecks to some two million unemployed. They were soon busy cutting down diseased apple trees, building airports and golf courses, straightening road curves, and restoring historic sites as well as decaying footbridges and camping areas in public parks and forest preserves. The CWA employed over four million through the winter, thereby transferring to federal agencies much of the relief problem which had overwhelmed local communities during the previous three years.

But there were still over ten million unemployed, and the NRA was not reaching them. Even one of the Federal Reserve bulletins had referred, in October 1933, to the slowing down of activity in industries "in which processing taxes or codes have become effective recently." Johnson struck back with characteristic vigor, insisting that this was not true, except in steel.

In Washington and elsewhere, dissatisfaction with the NRA and the General spread among conservatives as well, but not because of Johnson's dictatorial tone and methods. In all of the Wall Street area in New York below Fulton Street, only three Blue Eagles were observed in windows, despite the fact that brokerage houses and banks had signed NRA codes. Nevertheless, the December convention of the National Association of Manufacturers endorsed the NRA, though with considerable reservation.

As Roosevelt spoke confidently of the country's being on a steady march to better days, General Electric's President Gerard Swope proposed that the NRA be supplanted in its administrative functions by a super-organization of industry representatives, under the auspices of the Chamber of Commerce, which would administer new codes and provide for industrial self-rule. He felt that the existing codes were "unenforceable" and had led to extensive "chiseling." On the other hand, after their ninety-day testing period, steel-industry spokesmen requested a six-month extension of the steel code. Despite the recent decline in operating schedules and business, steel industrialists concluded that there had been significant increases in employment (92,000 men added) and in payrolls (up by nine million dollars) which warranted continuation of the code. No specific mention was made, however, of the increase in profits for management.

As the nation prepared to celebrate its first Christmas under the New Deal, the President issued an Executive Order which turned out to be more an appeal than a directive. Cautioning against a letdown in the drive for recovery, he extended the Reemployment Agreement to May 1, 1934, invited employers not yet under their own industry code to continue under the Blue Eagle, and predicted that by January 1, 1934, 70 percent of the nation's workers would be under industry-wide codes.

Summing up the year's accomplishments in the most laudatory terms, Johnson insisted that 24 million Americans had been aided by NRA, and 4 million rehired. The 180 codes then in operation had cut the hours of labor, raised the pay of millions, and abolished child labor and "homework." But he was particularly proud of NRA's contributions to the cotton-textile industry. His purported success, however, was short-lived. Cotton-textile workers, as well as some academicians, were soon demonstrating their revulsion at the role of industrial management and the NRA staff in perverting the humane objectives of the NIRA.

In Washington, William Green disclosed that while the outlook was brighter than the previous March, at least a half million workers had lost their jobs during the recession in November alone, and over ten million workers were still without industrial employment. The situation would have been far more critical if not for the CWA. While the millions who had been rehired since the President's inaugural were of course better off now than before, those already employed at more than a minimum wage had generally lost ground because of significant increases in the prices of food, clothing, and furnishings.

In the academic world, storm signals were raised. A prestigious group of economists and sociologists from across the country, assembled by Columbia University's President Nicholas Murray Butler, generally praised the New Deal. However, the group warned against the NRA policy of curbing production. Prosperity, these academicians insisted, depended upon increases in both purchasing power and production. And a general rise in prices was not, in and of itself, a sign of expanding prosperity.

From across the Atlantic, economist John Maynard Keynes joined the growing swell of criticism when he insisted that the NRA had been put across too hastily "in the false guise of being part of the technique of recovery." Though the social gains derived from the NRA were considerable, he could not detect any material gains leading to recovery. He criticized the raising of prices "by deliberately increasing prime costs or by restricting output . . . ," and added that the setback that American recovery experienced in the autumn had been predictable.

Raymond Moley, who had parted with the New Deal administration some months earlier to head a new weekly journal, and economists Irving Fisher of Yale and Willford I. King of New York University, sought to refute Keynes's major criticisms. While the professors felt obliged to concede that NRA had, at times, hindered economic recovery, Moley insisted that FDR had done most of what Keynes had suggested.

Johnson and his colleagues had made so many mistakes, and surrendered to industrial control so many times during the early months of the NRA, that they would have done well to suspend all price-fixing and output-restricting clauses before the end of 1933, and start all over again.

By the end of 1933, there was no order in the recovery picture, for there was no effective or responsible planning body for the NRA.

New York Times, October 28, November 2, December 9, 30, 1933, January 1, February 5, 1934; Robert MacIver, ed., *Economic Reconstruction. Report of the Columbia University Commission* (New York, 1934).

The Muted Voice of the Consumer

Within weeks of their appointment in late June 1933, it became clear to members of the Consumers' Advisory Board that a significant rise in the price of consumer goods had eaten away most earlier gains in consumer purchasing power. In mid-August, the first major defection occurred when William F. Ogburn, economics professor at the University of Chicago, resigned as a director of the consumers' group with a public blast against Johnson. Fearful of what might happen by the end of the year, when the nation's economy traditionally grew worse, and troubled by the General's persistent refusal to approve his suggestions for consumer representation, inspection of account books, quality standards, and purchasing-power indices, Ogburn warned that consumer interests were not safeguarded, and that the great experiment was doomed to failure. To protect consumers, improve the economy, and put people back to work, the establishment of price and purchasing power indices, as a minimum, was long overdue. Instead, in an action typical of the behavior which Ogburn lamented in Johnson and his key deputies, the NRA's Washington office had recently relegated consumer complaints to a new group which was totally unequipped to learn the facts about costs and prices, the subjects of most grievances. The result was that the role of the Consumers' Advisory Board was reduced to that of an ineffectual observer.

By his public blast, Ogburn sought to alert the President to some of the major weaknesses of the early NRA. Unfortunately, the Chief Executive permitted Johnson to ignore Ogburn, and to bypass any governmental group which questioned his decisions and direction.

But the Consumers' Advisory Board would not be entirely silenced. Gradually, it became part of a small consumer-minded opposition within the NRA, allied primarily with economic academicians in the Research and Planning Division. And it exerted some influence, in a manner which Johnson had not anticipated and did not welcome.

Headed by Mary Rumsey, the daughter of railroad magnate E. H. Harriman, and a close friend of Frances Perkins, the Board consisted of members who were varied in their economic outlook but united in their opposition to the type of price and production controls which Johnson and his deputies had fostered. The Board responded to price complaints by issuing memoranda and policy statements criticizing the damaging concessions to industry, and assailed many of the proposed codes as detrimental to the consumer. Although the Board failed to develop a viable consumer constituency with the power to effect policy changes, its statistics, challenges to existing policy, and suggestions of alternative goals helped sustain an independent, critical voice among progressive lawmakers, journalists, and civic spokesmen.

The Consumers' Advisory Board disclosed cases of prices being raised by enormous percentages, and of identical bids which indicated collusion among industrialists and wholesalers; it found codes fostering price-fixing, limitations of industrial output, and the allocation of quotas to inefficient plants; and it exposed padded items of cost that penalized efficient units—all at the expense of the consumer.

By November 1933, as disenchantment with the NRA spread, Johnson bowed to persistent demands of the Board for public hearings on the price question. Originally scheduled for early December, they were postponed to January 1934 at the behest of Christmas-minded merchants who feared their impact upon seasonal sales. At a meeting with the General on December 17, a consumers' delegation headed by Mary Rumsey and Leon Henderson of the Russell Sage Foundation protested the delay and, more importantly, underscored the harm being done the consumer by NRA codes. During this famous "shouting interview," when a doubting, bullying, Johnson suddenly met his match in an enraged Henderson, the NRA administrator roared, "If you're so goddamned smart, why don't you come down here and be my assistant on consumer problems?"

To the General's subsequent dismay, Henderson accepted the job and became one of the most effective critics of NRA's "business-oriented price and production policies." In February 1934, Henderson was designated head of the Research and Planning Division, and he revitalized this group of economists, whose key work had been sabotaged by his immediate predecessor, a former sales manager for General Motors. Although ineffective in the early policy-making era of NRA, by 1934 the statistical reporting, data, and recommendations of the Consumers' Advisory Board, and of the Research and Planning Division had a growing impact upon Johnson, and were facilitating a modest reorientation in trade-practice policy.

From the other end of Pennsylvania Avenue came increasingly effective Congressional blasts against Roosevelt's NRA. On January 3, the opening day of the 1934 session of Congress, progressive Republican Senator Gerald P. Nye of North Dakota charged that the NRA had fostered a monopoly in the electric-light-bulb industry headed by General Electric. When independent lamp manufacturers sought a redress of their grievances, their pleas were rejected by the National Electric Manufacturers Association, which was also the code authority for the industry. Within hours after Nye hurled these charges from the Senate floor, a defensive Richberg conceded their validity. But the fault, he maintained, lay with one of his assistants in permitting this development, not with general NRA policy.

Renewed attacks by Senators Borah and Nye fell like sledge-hammer blows, for they were now joined by two Democrats, conservative Carter Glass of Virginia and progressive Edward P. Costigan of Colorado. Pinpointing the haste and ineptitude with which NRA codes had been developed, Nye denounced many of them as "swindles upon the consumer." He demanded that the NRA cease being "an aid of monopoly," and that Johnson call a halt to his usual bombast.

In a personal address to a joint Congressional meeting, opening the new legislative session, Roosevelt had sought unsuccessfully to blunt the increasing attacks on the NRA. Viewing recovery as well under way, and the New Deal as here to stay, the President was unconvincing when he advised the congressmen that he was committed to preventing combinations "in furtherance of monopoly and in restraint of trade."

Shortly thereafter, an Executive Order directed that all aid be given to the "little man," and that no NRA code be used for price-fixing and discrimination. The Chief Executive insisted he was upholding the antitrust law—an assertion which was somewhat confusing in light of the law's circumvention by the NIRA —and decreed that an individual who was injured by unfair business practices under the NRA, and was dissatisfied with the way his grievance was handled by the regional or Washington offices of the organization, could press the case before the Federal Trade Commission or invoke the aid of the Department of Justice. This was a rather unrealistic position for the President to assume, in

view of the long delays and expense involved in the adjudication of disputes for the average aggrieved buyer of retail goods.

New York Times, August 15, December 16, 17, 1933; January
19, 20, 21, 23, 1934; Hawley, *The New Deal and the Problem of
Monopoly,* 75–78; Persia Campbell, *Consumer Representation in
the New Deal* (New York, 1940), 11, 28, 31, 35–36, 38–44, 46–51,
56–58, 60–61, 66–67; Lyon et al., *The National Recovery Administration,* 126–28, 131, 564–65, 706; Schlesinger, *The Coming of the
New Deal,* 129–31; William F. Ogburn in *Nation,* September 20,
1933, 318–20; T.R.B., in *New Republic,* October 18, 1933, 277.

The Public Is Invited to Protest

The intermittent memoranda and reports from the Consumers' Advisory Board proved invaluable to Senators Borah and
Nye, to newspapers, and to spokesmen of the protest movement
which swept the country. Seeking to deflate this criticism, Johnson convened the postponed public hearings on price grievances
in the Commerce Building on January 9, 1934.

But the hearings did not soften the opposition. Instead, the
testimony of aggrieved witnesses disclosed fatal weaknesses in
the organization, facilitated damaging denunciations from the
floor of the Senate, stimulated modifications in NRA policy, and
hastened the eventual downfall of the General. Innumerable cases
were cited by public and institutional purchasing agents, large
retailers, farm organizations, and consumer groups of prices
raised by enormous percentages and then standardized, of the
elimination of competitive safeguards, and of a pattern of identical contract bids which indicated collusion by steel manufacturers in the East, paper wholesalers in the Pacific Northwest,
and textile, printing, cement, and bituminous-coal industrialists
throughout the nation. In over a thousand pages of testimony,
witness after witness contended that the open-price provision
written into many of the codes—which required the public post-
ing throughout an industry of proposed price changes, generally
with waiting periods before the new prices could go into effect—

facilitated a decided trend toward monopolistic price-fixing, insured uniformity of price quotations, and illustrated the true nature of self-government in industry.

Primed with individual complaints from consumers, and prepared to present an overall appraisal of the impact of many of the codes discussed, the Consumers' Advisory Board was unexpectedly notified by Arthur D. Whiteside, Johnson's close subordinate and the presiding officer at the hearings, that in response to business objections, he had decided not to permit the Board to make public its report. This was not the first time that the Board's findings had been suppressed by Johnson and his staff, and although this latest gag rule was revoked prior to the hearings' conclusion, the harm had been done and additional ammunition afforded Borah, Nye, and other antitrusters.

One of the major conclusions emanating from this first set of hearings was that neither Johnson, Richberg, nor any other NRA official had provided for a serious study of open pricing. As a result, there was no organizational consensus concerning its impact on the market.

In the Senate, meanwhile, Nye and Borah intensified their attacks on Johnson and the NRA. According to Nye, the codes had become a cloak for the use of monopolistic practices which penalized and even eliminated small competitors. Senator Borah, a self-proclaimed spokesman for small business, insisted that only if the antitrust laws were restored, to operate in conjunction with the NIRA, could the Administration establish fair competition and protect labor, the consumer, and the small businessman.

As a result of the increasing protests, at least three significant developments occurred within the next few weeks. They added up to an endeavor by Johnson to alter policy, and an attempt by Roosevelt to placate Republican progressives whom he sought for his New Deal coalition.

On January 25, 1934, an NRA office order was issued staying or eliminating "open-price associations" in all codes not yet approved, pending a study of the question, for the first time, by the Consumers' Advisory Board, the Research and Planning Division, the Legal Division, and the Industrial Advisory Board. Thus, the consumer group, ineffective in the NRA's early development, seemed to have cleared the stage for critics of the codes by January 1934. However, within hours of Johnson's latest decree concerning "open-price associations," sudden protests from the business-oriented deputy administrators in the NRA, and from trade-association executives, inspired the General to backtrack and all but withdraw his original order.

Second, after six weeks of highly publicized negotiations with Senator Nye to head off a full-scale Congressional investigation of monopolistic tendencies in NRA codes, Johnson agreed to the creation by Roosevelt of a National Recovery Review Board. In a "moment of total aberration," as the General subsequently put it, he conceded to the new board's being chaired by the renowned trial lawyer Clarence Darrow, and accepted most of Nye's suggestions for board membership. The task of the new Review Board was to appraise the operations of the codes as they related to possible monopolistic developments, to examine their impact upon the small businessman, and to suggest improvements of NRA policies.

The third event, which intensified the rising public clamor against the NRA, was the Field Day of Criticism convened by Johnson on February 27, 1934. The Consumers' Advisory Board helped set the tone for the Field Day of Criticism through the wide publicity which accompanied issuance of its report, *Suggestions for Code Revision,* on February 19. The Board's conclusion, which was based upon analyses of prices and of administrative abuses in seven industries, was that the identification under open-price systems of the person or firm quoting the low price facilitated the use of pressure to force this price up to the level generally desired in the industry. Thus, self-government in industry was served, "cutthroat" competition was eliminated, and monopolistic practices were furthered. Resulting increases in prices to the ultimate consumer ranged from a low of 17 percent for coal to a high of 250 percent for copper hot-water boilers.

Johnson reacted negatively, and did nothing. The major thrust of the Consumers' Advisory Board indictment, however, was sustained a month later by the Federal Trade Commission. The FTC's report on the steel industry, issued pursuant to an earlier Senate resolution sponsored by Borah, appeared on March 19. It was severe in its criticism of the basing-point and price-reporting systems embodied in the steel code. According to the FTC, they tended to foster price-fixing and monopolistic practices which, in turn, insured domination of the steel industry by the two giants, United States Steel and Bethlehem Steel. This report further made clear that the FTC's conceptions of what constituted the "monopolistic practices" which the NIRA had debarred did not coincide with those of the General, Richberg, or their deputies.

Lyon et al., *The National Recovery Administration,* 706–9; Campbell, *Consumer Representation,* 48, 70–73, 74; *New York Times,* January 10, 11, 13, 19, 20, 21, 25, February 3, 7, 8, 20, 21, 22, March 5, 21, 22, May 31, 1934; Hawley, *The New Deal and the Problem of Monopoly,* 79–81; *Congressional Record* (73d Cong., 2d sess.), LXXVIII, 866, 870–77, 1075–86, 1442–44, 1824–25, 2156–58, 2945–46; Johnson, *The Blue Eagle,* 272; Johnson to FDR, December 13, 1933, and FDR to Johnson, December 18, 1933, Roosevelt Papers, OF 466; Baird, *Price Filing Under NRA Codes,* 453–58.

Field Day of Criticism

The outpouring of public witnesses anxious to testify against the NRA on the Field Day of Criticism, obliged the General to extend it for four days. Representatives of organized labor, consumers, retail merchandising organizations, and small businessmen and industry, swamped NRA deputies, often at five simultaneous meetings.

Before the two thousand men and women who overflowed the opening meeting at the Department of Commerce auditorium on February 27, Johnson conceded at once that mistakes had been made in the extraordinary task of codifying American industry in the short space of nine months. But he insisted that the NRA had been correct in its original estimate as to the number of men and women it would put back to work, and the extent to which it would increase mass purchasing power. In characteristic vein, he attacked the enemies of the Blue Eagle campaign as those who opposed higher wages and shorter hours, and then announced that he was about to embark on a new, twelve-point program to improve the NRA and its compliance machinery. But he was whistling in the dark. Only a few weeks before, he had been forced to beg retailers to "Keep prices down. For God's sake, keep prices down." This plea had been to no avail, for the NRA's compliance machinery had broken down; and organized labor had consequently become alienated from the business-oriented administrator.

Though repeating some of the criticism presented at the hearings in January, retail merchandisers protested, in particular, the impact of manufacturers' codes upon distributors, and of the measures intended to limit production, as well as the provisos to fix prices. As quantity buyers and representatives of federal, state, city, and college agencies pointed out, many industries employed the open-price list to insure inordinate and unjustified increases. Besides checking unfair competition, the use of the lists went a long way toward eliminating all competition, for the circulation of quotations within an industry tended to cause prices to become not only high but uniform. This uniformity was illustrated by data presented by E. J. Condon of Sears, Roebuck and Company, speaking for the Mail Order Association of America. He cited wholesale prices for a variety of standardized products in at least three different industries—gloves, wire screen cloth, and rubberized fabrics—to show the unyielding uniformity in quotations from any number of manufacturers.

The high level at which prices tended to be fixed was also demonstrated by some detailed price data collected by the Mail

Order Association for key lines of products over a period of nine years.

Index of Prices

	1924	1926	1929	1933
No Code, or Codes Free of Price Provisions	108.2	100.0	88.2	82.7 [1]
Approved Codes with Open-Price Provisions	101.2	100.0	90.2	111.2
Approved Codes with Outright Price-Fixing Provisions	100.8	100.0	95.3	98.6 [1]
Farm Products (U. S. Dept. of Labor)	——	100.0	——	55.9 [2]

1. December 15.
2. December 16.

Within six months of the start of the NRA, and with farm prices at little more than half of their 1926 level, prices quoted for products under open-price provisions were 11.2 percent higher than in 1926, and 21 percent above those of prosperous 1929. Open prices, apparently, had led to greater heights than outright price-fixing.

Mary E. O'Connor, director of purchase in the Division of Standards and Purchase of New York State, characterized the situation as one in which "the abuse of the so-called open-price association . . . is so well known that it might well be labelled disgraceful." Advertising for bids was a farce, since all prices were identical. Mrs. O'Connor produced a list of requirements on file with her division in Albany, amounting to ten million dollars. This potential purchasing power, she said, was frozen, and at least half of it would remain frozen indefinitely, "so long

as NRA codes are being used as a cloak to disguise illegal, unethical and unfair combinations in restraint of trade." She assured the hearing board that many other states were in a similar
predicament, and for months had been buying only absolutely
essential requirements because of their inability to obtain fair
bids.[1]

Elinore M. Herrick, vice chairman of the New York Regional Labor Board, and Mary Dewson, representing the National Consumers League, spoke of industrialists who took
advantage of the codes to break down decent standards. They
hired "learners" at less than minimum wages, and used them
to avoid the steady employment of workers; lowered wages of
skilled workers toward the minimums established by the codes;
resorted to increased use of the stretch-out or speed-up system,
particularly in cotton textiles; and made some wage earners
"executives" to escape limitations on working hours. It was
also pointed out that the effect of setting a lower minimum wage
for women in more than one-fourth of the codes was to discriminate against the female and insure cheap labor in competition with the men, with their higher pay.

The most highly publicized attack against the NRA and
Johnson's leadership was made by Cornelia Pinchot, outspoken
wife of Pennsylvania's progressive Republican governor. During
her recent tour of steel and textile towns in the Keystone State,
a number of her scheduled meetings in Bethlehem, Duquesne,
and other municipalities had been suddenly canceled by school
boards and local authorities, apparently at the behest of industrial management. Indicting the large steel companies for
flouting the labor provisions of the Recovery Act, and characterizing the work of the compliance bodies as a farce, she
asserted that many of the workers who had spoken with her on
the streets had been "turned in" by foremen and industrial
agents or labor spies and dismissed by steel-mill employers.
"Until men like Mr. Weir and Mr. Budd are made to obey the

1. *New York Times,* March 1, 1934.

law," she insisted, "I see no sense in taking the Blue Eagle away from a little beauty shop or small restaurant."

The workers she talked with still had faith in the President, but they felt that they had been betrayed by those whose task it was to secure compliance with law. In her highly charged testimony, she reminded the General that he had told the national convention of the AF of L, the previous October, that there was no longer any need to strike, for the NRA would protect the men in their right to organize:

> I wonder if General Johnson ever stays up nights and sees the faces of the people who are jobless and without resources, who went ahead and organized as allowed by the law and lost their jobs. I wonder what the workers think when they see Weir openly defying the United States government and getting away with it; when they see the case against him go to the Department of Justice and then back to the National Labor Board [see p. 100], and nothing issues but a silence so dramatic it has almost shaken their faith in the United States government.[2]

Stung by Cornelia Pinchot's personal indictment, the General was moved to reply that the NRA did not control the National Labor Board, nor police powers in Pennsylvania towns. He suggested she take the matter up with her husband, the Governor.

Lyon et al., *The National Recovery Administration,* 711–12; Johnson, *The Blue Eagle,* 295; Jonathan Mitchell in *New Republic,* March 21, 1934, 149–50; *New York Times,* February 27, March 1, 2, 3, 1934.

". . . we is only one-third living."

Another speaker at the Field Day of Criticism was John P. Davis, an unsung hero representing twenty-two black organizations associated with the Joint Committee on National Recovery, who offered innumerable instances of NRA codes being harshly discriminatory against minorities in general, and blacks

2. *New York Times,* March 1, 1934.

in particular, especially in the cotton-textile, laundry, shipping, and hotel and restaurant trades. Virtually nothing was noted of his testimony in American newspapers. To a nation which devoted little attention to the tragic ills inflicted upon its minority communities, the findings of Davis, and of W. E. B. Du Bois, Walter White, Roy Wilkins, and other black spokesmen should have been of major import. Unfortunately, Johnson, Richberg, the NRA staff, and organized labor, too, remained indifferent to the plight of black and minority workers.

The economy was in critical straits in the South, where the greater number of blacks lived prior to the Second World War. People were so poor, blacks in particular, that wages were spent instantaneously. Through the winter months of 1933–34, the South had been sustained primarily by federal money obtained largely through the AAA and the CWA. The latter poured out millions with a minimum of red tape, while the former distributed more than 100 million dollars in its cotton-crop-reduction program. But by resorting to various pretexts, the landlords and creditors of the poor saw to it that most of the disbursements of the AAA never reached the hands of tenant farmers and sharecroppers. The result was that millions of blacks and poor whites were living below any subsistence level. Before the end of the New Deal, hundreds of thousands of these unfortunate Southerners were turned adrift by an AAA which discriminated in favor of large landed proprietors.

What happened to the black industrial worker under the NIRA? Immediately prior to its enactment, more than 20 percent of all black workers were without jobs. The slightest rise in retail prices, without a concurrent increase in wages and reemployment, meant catastrophe for blacks, for their consumption then sank below the starvation level to which it had fallen in the previous four years.

Neither the craft-minded AF of L, nor the New Deal administration, exhibited much concern for black or minority workers during this period. Despite the fact that the great majority of black wage earners were blue-collar workers, they were rarely found in the ranks of organized labor during the early years of the New Deal. At least nineteen independent unions excluded blacks from membership, an additional ten admitted them only to segregated locals, while many others prohibited black membership by tacit consent.

Since most black workers were either semiskilled or unskilled, they played a very minor role in those craft unions which did admit them. And while some trade unions responded to Section 7a with the greatest organizing drives in history, the overwhelming bulk of those in the AF of L did little or nothing to include blacks in these campaigns. Instead, black workers found themselves displaced by whites at the specific behest of the Brotherhood of Electrical Workers and the Building Service Employees' in New York, and by other AF of L unions in Milwaukee, St. Louis, and elsewhere throughout the nation. In view of American labor history, black workers had no reason to trust organized labor. The closed shop, to them, usually meant jobs for white unionists only. Thus, many black workers and community spokesmen were not unhappy that the Recovery Act had established only ineffective machinery to enforce collective-bargaining provisions. How could they feel otherwise when, for example, the NAACP was convinced that "practically every important entry that the Negro has made into industries previously closed to him has been through his activity as a strikebreaker"?

With only 3 percent of the 1,500,000 black industrial workers in AF of L national unions, almost half of them members of the Brotherhood of Sleeping Car Porters, they were helpless to counter the demands of Southern management for longer hours and lower wages for those occupations and industries in which the predominant labor supply was black. With rare exception, black workers had no power with which to bargain collectively. Since less than one-third of all black workers were in the skilled category, and the craft-oriented AF of L national leadership was unwilling to persuade member unions to remove exclusion clauses from their constitutions and admit blacks to membership, it was inevitable that black workers and their community spokesmen would view organized labor as their enemy.

Any improvements of labor conditions among blacks, therefore, would arise exclusively from the NRA codes, the first opportunity being in the cotton-textile industry. Wholly unorganized blacks were excluded from skilled occupations by labor and management, and were generally employed, if at all, as outside crew gangs and helpers, the lowest-paid workers in the industry. Only a substantial reduction in their hours of work would facilitate increased black employment, and only an increase in the wage rates in these occupations would insure greater buying power. Unfortunately, the textile code, which became effective on July 17, 1933, made no provisions for reduction of the hours or increase in the wages of outside crews and cleaners. Not until six months later was any consideration given to these occupational groups; at that time the industry did propose a wage-and-hour scale for these exempted classes. But meanwhile, the price of flour, cornmeal, lard, and similar commodities sold at company-owned stores in the South had skyrocketed by an average of 30 percent.

After suffering starvation wages six months longer than any other class, and being paid at a rate much lower than that of any other group in the industry, the outside crews among the cotton-textile workers learned early in 1934 that the NRA had finally issued an order which dealt directly with them. Without a public hearing, and without affording any labor representatives the opportunity to present their case, the NRA created wage scales which provided that outside crews and cleaners should get 75 percent of the minimum wage already set, and work four hours beyond the maximum weekly hour scale then in operation. Thus, for those with the greatest proportion of unemployed, the reduction in hours was far less than for the more fortunate groups. And the established minimum wage would generally, in the absence of any collective-bargaining power, become the maximum wage.

The brunt of this type of discrimination was borne by blacks. And even though the nine-dollar-a-week minimum meant an increase in wages in some mills, for large numbers of blacks in other mills—near Greensboro, North Carolina—for example, this minimum was less than what they had received during the worst period of the depression. Furthermore, in view of the heightened prices in company stores, any wage raises that did occur amounted, in terms of increased purchasing power, to virtually nothing.

The full impact of this decision was yet to unfold, for it not only served as a precedent in the setting of the wage scale for twenty thousand black workers in other branches of the textile industry but was used to the advantage of employers in more than thirty other NRA codes of fair competition. Further study of the codes disclosed that wherever the predominant labor supply of a geographical section was black, that section was automatically classified as Southern and given the lowest wage rate. Proponents of a North-South differential openly conceded, at numerous code hearings, that the presence of blacks in an area insured a lower wage rate for that region.

Despite appeals to NRA economists not to grade workers on the basis of efficiency, and reminders that the original objective of the NIRA was to establish a minimum wage rate that would provide for more than a bare living for all workers, regardless of relative efficiency, Johnson and Richberg endorsed the concept of geographical wage differentials, basing their justification on the inefficiency of industrial workers in the South—by which they really meant the inefficiency of black workers. Although unsupported by any serious research findings, NRA spokesmen remained adamant in their belief that black labor was inherently inefficient.

Discriminated against by NRA codes, blacks also found themselves denied equitable treatment by NRA compliance machinery in the South. Originally composed primarily of members of chambers of commerce or their equivalents, many of whom turned out to be code violators, local compliance boards made no serious endeavor to protect black complainants from subsequent discrimination or discharge. One cotton-garment employer in Arkansas, for example, fired 194 black girls because he could not discover the name of the worker who complained of his paying only $6.16 a week, instead of the code minimum of $12. Those discharged did not receive any back pay, and no action was taken by the NRA against the employer. The situation was not noticeably altered, at least for blacks, even after enforcement of compliance had been placed in the hands of NRA employees. In fact, as it entered its second year of operation, the NRA did not employ a single black with a rank equal to that of a clerk. And Johnson had once stated that it would be simply "preposterous" to have a study of black labor made by a Northern black.

The evasion of NRA regulations was so widespread that there was no decrease in the wage spread between white and black labor. In fact, after months of study, a subcommittee of white representatives from the Department of Labor and the NRA and three blacks—Eugene Jones, Robert Weaver, and Forrester Washington—concluded that during the NRA period "the spread in total income . . . between southern white labor as a whole and southern Negro labor as a whole has been increased."

A key white aide reported to Interior Secretary Ickes that the seeming lack of concern by Johnson and the NRA staff with the problems of black workers had "caused much dissatisfaction among Negroes, and the officials of the NRA have made no serious attempt to acquaint themselves with the problems of the Negro population and particularly with the problems of the Negro laboring population caused by the operation of the NRA."

As John P. Davis had indicated at the public hearings in Washington, black industrial workers had the right to hope that their inferior economic status would at least not be aggravated by the NRA. Instead, there was not a section of the country where blacks had not suffered because of the Blue Eagle. That symbol had become for them a "black hawk, a predatory bird which makes prices go up but not their wages, which makes them lose their jobs, which weakens their economic position." For blacks, the letters *NRA* had but one meaning—"Negroes Ruined Again." Was it any wonder that Du Bois and others lashed out in bitter condemnation of Hugh Johnson and his organization with remarks like, "The most sinister power that the NRA has reinforced is the American Federation of Labor"?

While the record-breaking organizational drives of the AF of L benefited hundreds of thousands of white workers, they generally drove blacks out of skilled jobs everywhere. Black spokesmen saw Southern employers thumbing their noses at NRA compliance machinery and insisting they would not pay code wages to blacks. As one black worker said to John Davis, "Before the Blue Eagle we was just one-half living, but now we is only one-third living."

New York Times, March 1, 1933; John P. Davis, "Blue Eagles and Black Workers," *New Republic,* November 14, 1934, 7–9; Raymond Wolters, "Section 7a and the Black Worker," *Labor History,* X (Summer 1969), 459–74; Raymond Wolters, *Negroes and the Great Depression: The Problem of Economic Recovery* (Westport, Conn., 1970), 83–90, 140–48, 149–55, 169–87.

The Prospects Are Hopeless

Summing up briefly at the conclusion of the Field Day of Criticism, Johnson promised the impossible: to convey the essence of the sweeping indictments of the NRA, and the scores of suggestions for fundamental revision, to the NRA Code Authority Conference, of some four thousand code-authority and code-committee members, convening in Washington two days later. The Field Day had all but buried the NRA, and no magician, not even the General, could revive it in 1934.

Proceedings at the gathering of pro-management businessmen merely confirmed the overwhelming obstacles confronting Johnson, and the impossibility of regaining the initiative in the face of rising Congressional, press, and public opposition. In response to the President's urgent appeal for "immediate cooperation" to facilitate increased wages, shorter hours, and expanded employment, and the General's proposal for a 10 percent reduction in working hours and a 10 percent increase in wages, these shortsighted businessmen could only visualize economic disaster. Their concern, instead, was with problems of bureaucratic organization, such as excessive slowness in dealing with "chiselers," frequent shifts in NRA policy, and frustrating confusion from the overlapping of codes. They completely rejected the harsh attacks against the open-price provision, and the many recommendations for consumer relief presented at the Field Day of Criticism.

Johnson's appointment of study committees at the conclusion of this pro-business conference was a meaningless gesture. He had already received more than enough reports and studies from his own Research and Planning Division, the Consumers' Advisory Board, the Compliance Division, and the Federal Trade Commission, and soon would be getting the Darrow Report, all verifying the destructive nature of developing cartels, of the monopolistic implications of the open-price plans, and of the breakdown in enforcement. Even National Emergency Council meetings affirmed a state of demoralization, lack of consistent direction, and serious internal conflict within the NRA.

Within the week after the Field Day of Criticism, the sixth meeting of the National Emergency Council was held in the Cabinet Room of the White House. Members of the presidential Cabinet, along with spokesmen of key administrative agencies, were convened at a typical gathering to hear confidential reports concerning NRA developments around the country. What they were shown was a cross section of deteriorating conditions within the recovery program, as reported by state directors of the National Emergency Council. Many were extremely critical of ineffective administration, in spite of some momentary improvement resulting from the Code Authority Conference, and the critical forum which preceded it.

It was generally conceded that the great breakdown in compliance with NRA provisions nationally was the result of a conflict of authority among administrative officials in Washington. The NRA office manager in Maine reported, for example, that the only instruction received by the state director of the Civil Works Administration was to accept the lowest bid offered, with no reference being made to NRA code compliance. The state director for the NEC from Arizona indicated that the purchasing agent for the CWA in his state was accepting the offers of the lowest bidders, even though it was known that they were not fulfilling NRA stipulations. In Vermont and elsewhere, the United States Army was awarding contracts for shoe repairs and lumber to non-NRA firms, or those whose prices were below the code minimum.

Contractors coming to Washington immediately found themselves ensnarled by conflicting rules and regulations offered by the Public Works Administration and the War Department. For example, War Department contracts required compliance with the approved applicable code, while the Adjutant General of the Army issued an order to all special bases advising them that the Comptroller General had ruled that the price-posting and purchasing requirements of the codes did not apply to the United States government. Another federal agency included the code restrictions in its invitations to bid, yet enclosed in the same envelope a slip quoting the Comptroller General to the effect that bidders were not required to comply with NRA conditions.

These conflicts were illustrative of serious administrative dissension in the New Deal, and of differences which exacerbated a swiftly deteriorating condition within the NRA. They defied any attempts at coordination by such presidential endeavors as the National Emergency Council, or by the leadership of Johnson and Richberg.

Proceedings of the National Emergency Council, Meeting No. 6, March 6, 1934, as disclosed in Lester G. Seligman and Elmer E. Cornwell, Jr., eds., *New Deal Mosaic: Roosevelt Confers With His*

National Emergency Council, 1933–1936 (Eugene, Ore., 1965), 136–37, 141–43; Lyon et al., *The National Recovery Administration,* 712; Solomon Barkin, *NRA Work Materials 45-B-2, NRA Policies, Standards and Code Provisions on Basic Weekly Hours of Work* (Washington, D. C., 1936), 168–76; *New York Times,* March 3, 6–9, 16, 29, 1934.

4

Section 7a:
Labor's Magna Charta?
Part I

DESPITE general endorsement of the NRA code provisions, many large-scale employers refused to shelve their traditional hatred for trade unions. However, confronted with imminent collapse of the nation's economy—and having failed politically —industrial and business management were momentarily willing to concede the initiative to the New Deal. In return for exemption from the antitrust laws, much of industry grudgingly accepted its version of Section 7a. At the same time, the National Association of Manufacturers remained adamantly opposed to any concessions to labor, promising to "fight energetically against any encroachments by closed shop labor unions." Its response was to foster the company union, particularly in heavy industries, as a counterweight to organizing endeavors by the AF of L. The result was the greatest number of work stoppages since 1921.

On the very day that Roosevelt signed the NIRA, the Associated Press sent a dispatch from Youngstown, Ohio, which referred to the selection by 7,500 employees at Republic Steel of company-union representatives to act for them with respect to conditions affecting the workers and the company. A similar form of employee representation was announced almost simultaneously by Carnegie Steel in notices posted in its plants in

Youngstown and Pittsburgh. Both the Carnegie and Republic company-union plans were patterned after a system in effect at Bethlehem Steel and at Youngstown Sheet and Tube since 1918. As Robert P. Lamont, president of the Iron and Steel Institute, had warned Congress, steel management's response to Section 7a was the company union. In 1932, there had been only seven company unions in the industry; by 1934 there were over ninety.

Seeking to explain the hostile reaction of businessmen in general to the labor legislation of the New Deal era, particularly Section 7a, Robert E. Lane some years later indicated that the danger posed to them was not one of financial loss, necessarily, but of "cost in status, in conceptions of the self, in freedom to make certain traditional decisions, in the [possible] disruption of once familiar and stable areas of managerial discretion." The result of this reaction by businessmen was a continuation of the pre-1933 pattern of industrial relations—"discrimination against union workers, the use of espionage, the establishment of company unions, and a narrow construction of the representation and bargaining rights of trade union officials." [1]

John L. Lewis, Sidney Hillman, garment-union leader David Dubinsky, and even William Green, were equally adamant in their interpretation of Section 7a: that Congress intended the workers to join independent organizations, and that trade unions provided the obvious means through which employees could best bargain collectively.

Richberg had been appointed general counsel to the NRA because he had demonstrated a basic accord with Johnson and Moley, and because he had the confidence of the labor movement and its leadership. At the start, then, both the AF of L and industry viewed Richberg as the labor spokesman in the NRA bureaucracy. Johnson, however, had been more perceptive than labor in his appraisal of Richberg, for the two saw eye to eye in their interpretation of Section 7a.

Within weeks of his own appointment, Johnson berated both

1. Robert E. Lane, *The Regulation of Businessmen* (New Haven, Conn., 1954), 34–35.

labor leaders and industrial management: the former for insisting that workers could only benefit from the NRA by joining independent unions, the latter for contending that only company unions could help the worker. Seeking to adopt a neutral pose, Johnson insisted that it was not his purpose "to organize either industry or labor." From the start, however, Johnson veered strongly toward support of management's overall view of Section 7a. On August 14, he advised the Special Industrial Recovery Board, "This law should bring about open-shops where a man will be employed regardless of whether he belongs to any union or not." In a little more than a week, Richberg joined the General in issuing a joint policy statement in which they made clear that the representatives of the majority of workers in an industrial plant or business establishment could not speak on behalf of all the workers, and that individuals and minorities could do their own bargaining and agree on separate contracts. Furthermore, they insisted that Section 7a did not preclude the existence of company unions, as long as management did not resort to "interference, restraint or coercion."

Early on, Johnson and Richberg spoke out against the principle of majority rule in unionization, undermining the beneficial effects which labor leaders had wishfully anticipated from Section 7a's guarantees of the right to organize and bargain collectively. And acceptance of the company union by the NRA administrator and his general counsel enabled management to evade those very provisions of the law which purportedly protected independent labor organizations. The groundwork was thus quickly laid for an escalating dispute which ravaged organizational relations, toppled personal reputations, and destroyed the Recovery Administration.

Bernstein, *Turbulent Years,* 32; *New York Times,* June 17, 1933; Fine, *The Automobile Under the Blue Eagle,* 151; Moley, *The First New Deal,* 290; Johnson, *The Blue Eagle,* 201, 212; Schlesinger, *The Coming of the New Deal,* 146, 162–63; Johnson, NRA News Release No. 34, July 7, 1933; *New York Times,* August 24, 1933; Lyon et al., *The National Recovery Administration,* 462–

65; Lewis L. Lorwin and Arthur Wubnig, *Labor Relations Boards* (Washington, D. C., 1935), 51, 59–60, 73–76; Special Industrial Recovery Board, Proceedings of Meeting No. 9 (August 14, 1933), 9, in Record Group 9, Miscellaneous Reports and Documents, Series 39, Box 8462, National Archives.

In Union There Is Strength

Workers in mills, shops, and mines throughout the nation, with a new spirit and with courage awakened by Roosevelt and the passage of Section 7a, were willing to join trade unions by the hundreds of thousands. All they needed was the call from optimistic and imaginative leadership. Many workers had even been convinced that the AF of L unions were the "official" unions of the NRA. But only a limited number of astute labor leaders, such as those in the coal, men's-clothing, and ladies'-garment industries, were prepared to exploit Section 7a immediately and fully. By the mid-1930s, the craft unions were moribund. The newer industrial unions were an adaptation to the mold cast by the industrial corporations; they sought to organize all labor within an industry—the unskilled, the semiskilled, and the skilled —under one union banner. Lewis, Hillman, and Dubinsky hastened to organize the unorganized along these mass, industrial lines. They did not seek help from an outdated AF of L, from a volatile, industry-oriented Johnson, or from an increasingly conservative Richberg. The results were soon observable in membership figures which surpassed those for 1920, and in strong organizations and collective-bargaining agreements in the affected industries. By contrast, the weak unions which depended for sustenance upon a divided, craft-dominated AF of L leadership, or an NRA overwhelmed by management spokesmen and ideology, found little to cheer about during the early days of the New Deal.

DUBINSKY. Developments involving the socialist-led International Ladies' Garment Workers' Union (ILGWU) were characteristic. From a peak of 105,000 members in 1920, and after years of civil war with a Communist-led bloc, the ILGWU had, by early 1933, degenerated into a decaying union with 40,000 members spread thinly around the country. Working conditions were so bad that the dress-manufacturing and related industries in the key center of New York, and elsewhere, amounted to one huge sweatshop. Short, stocky Dubinsky, a conscientious activist, who had acquired his union and socialist background with the Bund (the General Jewish Workers Union) in Russian Poland, and in the prison camps of Siberia, had ascended from the ranks of Local 10 to become president of a bankrupt ILGWU in June 1932.

More a pragmatist than an ideologue, Dubinsky quickly realized the potentialities of the New Deal. Two months after Roosevelt's inaugural in March 1933, he went over to the offensive with the aid of young socialists and veteran union organizers, and successfully struck the non-union Philadelphia dress industry. He opened simultaneous organizing drives in sixty cities, and with the help of some socially conscious New York employers and Sidney Hillman, of the Labor Advisory Board, pushed through a comparatively enlightened NRA code for the women's coat-and-suit industry: child labor was prohibited, a work week of thirty-five hours for manufacturing employees and forty hours for nonmanufacturing employees was established, and wages were substantially raised.

On August 16, shortly before hearings commenced on their industry code, sixty thousand dress workers between New Haven, Connecticut, and Camden, New Jersey, responded to Dubinsky's call for a general strike. The garment industry in this area—including New York—was shut down solid. Three days later, industry spokesmen capitulated and the strike ended. The union not only more than tripled its membership in three days but increased wages significantly, established the closed shop and the thirty-five-hour work week, and forced the abolition of sweatshop conditions. This success was repeated in Chicago, Philadelphia, Fort Wayne, Minneapolis, Cleveland, Kansas City, Los Angeles, Boston, and even Montreal and Toronto. The terms of the settlement were shortly incorporated into an NRA code. Within a few months, the ILGWU was the third-largest union in the AF of L with some 200,000 members and all financial debts cleared.

Max D. Danish, *The World of David Dubinsky* (Cleveland, 1957), 75–82 and *passim;* Benjamin Stolberg, *Tailor's Progress* (Garden City, N. Y., 1944), 156–215; McAlister Coleman in *Nation,* May 7, 14, 1938, 525–27, 558–60; A. H. Raskin, "Dubinsky: Herald of Change," *Labor History,* special supplement (Spring 1968), 21; Bernstein, *Turbulent Years,* 77–89.

HILLMAN. Since the days in 1914 when he helped found and head the Amalgamated Clothing Workers of America, Sidney Hillman had been hailed as a pioneering "labor statesman" in the mainstream of American pragmatism. Well trained in his youth in Russian Lithuania as a socialist and an intellectual, with a Jewish seminary background, Hillman relied heavily on academicians for economic guidance. By 1933, he was particularly alert to the need for responding to the Great Depression on a national scale, through appropriate public policy and a revived labor movement. It was, therefore, natural for him to view Section 7a as a golden opportunity for labor, and for his weakened union in particular. Since 1929, Hillman and the Amalgamated had been helpless in the face of wage cutting, burgeoning sweatshops, and a decline in membership to 60,000 from a peak of 177,000 in 1920.

Immediately after enactment of the NIRA, Hillman set a pattern for the rest of the country when he successfully struck the men's-clothing industry in New York City and obtained wage increases ranging from 10 to 30 percent. The union next won victories in upstate New York, Boston, Philadelphia, Baltimore, Chicago, Milwaukee, St. Louis, and Rochester, an important men's-clothing center. Turning their endeavors to the cotton-garment industry (mainly shirts) on May 1, Amalgamated organizers swept through New York and smaller shops in outlying towns in Connecticut, New Jersey, and Pennsylvania. By the end of 1933, the union rolls had hurtled to some 125,000. As a member of the NRA's Labor Advisory Board, Hillman was able to push through the men's-clothing code, one of the first adopted, which raised wages significantly and reduced the work week from forty-four to thirty-six hours. The cotton-garment code was not as favorable, for the workers were less well organized.

Matthew Josephson, *Sidney Hillman: Statesman of American Labor* (Garden City, N. Y., 1952), 356–74 and *passim;* Jean Gould, *Sidney Hillman, Great American* (Boston, 1952), 282–96 and *passim;* A. H. Raskin, "Sidney Hillman, 1887–1946," *American Jewish Year Book,* XLIX (1947–48), 67–80; Charles A. Madison, *American Labor Leaders* (New York, 1950), Ch. XII; Bernstein, *Turbulent Years,* 66–77.

LEWIS. Within months, if not weeks, Dubinsky and Hillman had converted their decaying unions into powerful arms of a reviving labor movement. But the most dramatic figure of all was a labor leader who had supported Herbert Hoover in 1932. Massive, lumbering John L. Lewis, who had turned arch-conservative in the 1920s, firmly grasped the potential of Section 7a even before it became law. Throwing all of the union's remaining treasury, and over a hundred organizers and volunteers, into the campaign, Lewis' United Mine Workers swept through coalfields which had once been union strongholds, as well as those in which unionism had never existed. Thousands of union circulars advised miners that "the President wants you to join." Of course, they thought FDR was meant. But even these circulars seemed unnecessary, for workers streamed into the union en masse. The day after Roosevelt signed the NIRA, it was reported that 80 percent of Ohio's miners had signed membership cards. Two days later, West Virginia's anti-union Logan County was completely organized. And so it went in Kentucky, Pennsylvania, Colorado, and New Mexico. Within weeks, much of the coalfields had been organized by the UMW.

Tortured negotiations with mine management followed throughout the summer, as Lewis sought a national collective-bargaining agreement for the commercial mines, and then its implementation in the bituminous-coal code. In the process, Johnson became an irritating, almost fatal, obstacle when he threw himself needlessly into the collective-bargaining proceedings. As labor historian Irving Bernstein put it, Johnson "imposed upon the strained coal negotiations his own particular blend of bluster, bombast, Bourbon and baloney."

Finally, between September 16 and 21, 1933, with the help of Roosevelt, the bituminous-coal code was signed for commercial mines. A disappointment to many miners, the coal code did establish the eight-hour day, the forty-hour week, and the check-off of union dues, though not the closed shop. Payment in scrip was abolished, miners were no longer required to purchase food at the company store or live in a company house, and child labor (of those under seventeen) was forbidden. Historic progress had been made for brutally exploited workers.

More challenging was the attempt to establish collective bargaining in the captive mines, those owned by steel companies and producing coal for their consumption. Lewis demanded of the traditionally anti-union steel owners that they accept unchanged the terms of the commercial-mine settlement. Their backbones suddenly strengthened by economic indices which showed an upward trend through the spring, by the National Association of Manufacturers' issuance of its opposing interpretation of Section 7a, and by Richberg's willingness to exclude the checkoff of union dues as an issue for discussion, the steel owners' reply to Lewis was to expand company unionism and refuse to negotiate seriously. Eventually, on January 19, 1934, after a number of intervening procedural steps which involved the President in a helpful role, the ending of a crippling strike, employee elections in late November which were won largely by the UMW, and final arbitration by the National Labor Board, collective-bargaining agreements were reached for many of the captive mines. The accords approached, but did not equal in every detail, the provisions of the commercial-mine settlement. What was important was that the UMW had finally broken through one of the worst anti-union barriers in American industry.

Within a year of the NIRA's enactment, membership in the United Textile Workers of America approached the amazing figure of 250,000, with more than three hundred locals in the traditionally hostile South, seventy-four of them in the key state of North Carolina. Similar developments in the rubber, power, and electrical-equipment industries were often achieved over the opposition of the AF of L's Executive Council. On the other hand, too many conservative, old-line labor leaders could not liberate themselves from the fears and anxieties of the disastrous 1920s. As a result, they rejected industrial unionism until it was too late, found themselves following, instead of leading, the mass of unorganized workers, and became reluctantly involved in, and then all but overwhelmed by, debilitating controversies with a revivified industrial management, as well as with Johnson and Richberg. That large part of the labor movement which relied upon the NRA and its confused, overworked and at times hysterically driven administrator for sustenance and strength was afforded little encouragement.

Saul D. Alinsky, *John L. Lewis* (New York, 1949), 67–69; Schlesinger, *The Coming of the New Deal,* 105; Mary Van Kleech, *Miners and Management* (New York, 1934), 320–25; *New York Times,* July 27, 29, August 1, 4–6, 8, 9, 19, September 13, 15, October 3, 1933; Rosenman, ed., *The Year of Crisis,* 439–40; Bernstein, *Turbulent Years,* 37 66; James P. Johnson, "Drafting the NRA Code˙ of Fair Competition, for the Bituminous Coal Industry," *Journal of American History,* LIII (December 1966), 521–41.

Johnson on Equity and Mediation

Johnson was constantly at odds with elements of labor over interpretation of the law, or pledges broken. The General had seen nothing wrong in conceding to many a trade association exclusive responsibility for policing its own industry: serving as the code-authority board, it functioned with a government-sustained budget, and in the name of the NRA. Yet not until early December 1933, did Johnson finally bow to concerted pressure from organized labor and Perkins and agree to appoint labor representatives to some code-authority boards. Subsequently, Johnson did concede that government members of code authorities should have labor and consumer advisers, with access to official records and the right to be heard. But he never really implemented this policy, for he bowed to strong opposition from industrial leaders.

If there were any doubts about Johnson's basic attitudes toward organized labor, the AF of L leadership should have cast them aside after he addressed their convention in October 1933. At that time, he insisted that unions were no longer needed, and that strikes had become superfluous since the President had created new mediation machinery under the NRA. If unions persisted in maintaining their traditional role, they should at least be under government supervision. What did the General mean by "government supervision"? And what was this mediation machinery which he so proudly lauded as an alternative to unions?

Johnson to FDR, June 26, 1934, Roosevelt Papers, OF 466; *New York Times,* October 11, 1933; Hawley, *The New Deal and the Problem of Monopoly,* 89.

The Auto Code: Defeat for Labor

Given additional time by the President's Reemployment Agreement to secure the codification of business and industry, Johnson resorted to personal diplomacy to hasten action by the key industry—automobile manufacturing. When he met with industry representatives in Detroit on July 28, he not only clarified many troubling questions relating to Section 7a, but convinced them that "he was on the whole sympathetic with the industry's point of view."

While assuring employers that they could bargain individually with their men, he did remind them that they could not refuse to bargain with the chosen representatives of the workers. But Johnson set the stage for industry's victory when he concluded, "The fact that you bargain with the men doesn't mean you have to agree." Further, he conceded the group's interpretation of Section 7a—that the selection, retention, and advancement of employees would be "on the basis of individual merit without regard to their membership or nonmembership in any organization." Management now knew where Johnson stood, and how far they could go.

The deputy administrator designated on August 1 to supervise the prehearing conferences and the public hearings on the proposed automobile code was Robert W. Lea. The former president of an automobile company, and of the Moline Plow Company, with which his friend Johnson had been associated, Lea viewed economic problems through the eyes of the employer. Despite opposition from the Legal Division of the NRA, and from Green speaking in a dual capacity (for the Labor Advisory Board and the AF of L), the auto-industry representatives refused to be swayed from the main thrust of their open-shop interpretation of Section 7a. Vital support for industry's viewpoint came from Richberg, who testified that the selection and retention of employees on the basis of merit was "a proper construction of the law."

Although specific reference to the open shop was eventually dropped from the code, the merit clause remained, along with provisions for maximum hours and minimum wages which were agreeable to industry but not to the LAB. The latter maintained, and the deputy administrator conceded, that the proposed wages and hours would not result in the reemployment at satisfactory wages of a substantial portion of the jobless auto workers. A reluctant LAB meekly surrendered when it wired the President on August 26, shortly before he approved the code, that it was willing to accept the automobile code "with the understanding that no section or sentence contained therein modifies, qualifies, or changes Section 7a" and that the merit clause did "not establish a precedent to be followed in the preparation or acceptance of any other code."

Here was a solid victory for industry over the AF of L leadership and an anemic auto union. The code's minimum-wage scale affected few workers, the variations permitted in maximum hours meant industry retained flexibility in the handling of the labor force, while the merit clause insured that, in spite of Section 7a, industrial relations in the open-shop automobile industry remained unchanged. Other labor requests, such as a dismissal wage, overtime pay, and labor representation on the code authority, were rejected upon the insistence of the manufacturers. And no public consideration was given to questionable trade practices in the industry.

Since the AF of L union in the auto industry had not been able to get off the ground with its weak, unimaginative organizing drive, the auto magnates, and President Roosevelt, felt that they could simply ignore the reservations of Green and the LAB. Labor had no place to go, and Roosevelt sought industry's cooperation. Furthermore, in an act that exemplified the weakness of his leadership, and the ineffectiveness of the AF of L's conservative craft-union philosophy in the 1930s, Green had yielded to White House urgings that he eventually accept those reservations in the automobile code which seriously limited the application of Section 7a to the industry. This was not the last of Green's surrenders to Roosevelt.

By the end of August, as a partial result of the auto "settlement," twenty-nine proposed codes contained the merit clause, and President Harriman of the Chamber of Commerce recommended its incorporation in all codes, to safeguard the open shop. When the LAB warned of disaster facing the NRA if use of the merit clause was extended, Johnson, and then FDR, agreed that no further "interpretations" of Section 7a would henceforth be embodied in any code. Yet the merit clause was not eliminated from the automobile code when it was subsequently renewed. For the life of the NRA, the automobile manufacturers formulated and interpreted their own code, with the approval of the President.

Fine, *The Automobile Under the Blue Eagle,* 55, 60, 70–72.

Early Mediation Through the National Labor Board

During the tremendous upsurge, in the summer of 1933, of costly strikes, lockouts, and work stoppages, which at one time involved over 300,000 workers, the President was reminded by Green and others that the Recovery Act made no provision for the speedy settlement of such disputes. If the Administration's war on the Great Depression was to get off the ground, then something new had to be done to end these enervating struggles.

During the first week of August, the President adopted, in its exact wording, the recommendation of the Industrial and Labor Advisory Boards that he create a tripartite National Labor Board (NLB) of seven members—three from labor, three from industry, and—at its head—the public representative, New York's Senator Wagner.[2] This group was to "consider, adjust, and settle differences and controversies that may arise through differing interpretations of the President's Re-employment Agreement." (Employers subscribing to the Re-employment Agreement had agreed to observe Section 7a.) Employers and employees were "to take no disturbing action pending hearings and final decision." The NLB could establish local organizations to facilitate settlements.

Unfortunately, Roosevelt issued no Executive Order grant-

2. In addition to Wagner, the original members of the NLB were William Green, economics professor Leo Wolman, of Columbia University and the Labor Advisory Board, and John L. Lewis, for labor; and Walter C. Teagle, president of the Standard Oil Company of New Jersey and chairman of the Industrial Advisory Board, Gerard Swope, president of the General Electric Company, and Louis E. Kirstein, general manager of Filene's, Boston, for industry. Prof. William M. Leiserson of Antioch College was appointed executive secretary, with young Milton Handler, a specialist in antitrust law, as the General Counsel.

ing the NLB specific authority until mid-December. In the interim, the vagueness of Section 7a, which facilitated a flood of labor-management disputes, was matched by the vagueness of the decree which established the NLB. To this must be added the difficulties created by the Johnson-Richberg policy. The NLB had no defined procedures and no specific power of enforcement. The most the Board could do was ask the NRA to deprive a recalcitrant employer of the right to display the Blue Eagle; then the NRA-minded consumer—it was supposed —would refuse to purchase his products. It might also recommend that the Department of Justice look into possible violations of the law. However, despite the uncertainty of their position, Wagner and his colleagues on the NLB, interpreting liberally the original recommendation of the Industrial and Labor Advisory Boards, responded immediately and firmly in the NLB's first major test, a recognition strike in Reading, Pennsylvania, hosiery mills.

When the employers of the Berkshire Knitting Mills, a leader of the nonunion firms, refused to recognize the American Federation of Full-Fashioned Hosiery Workers after a whirlwind organizing drive, ten thousand workers went out on strike on July 5, 1933. On August 10, the newly created NLB invited representatives of the mills and the workers to convene in Washington. That same day, the NLB introduced the "Reading Formula," which established a Board pattern for settling strikes and laid the groundwork for a "common law" interpretation of Section 7a: The union called off the strike, and employees were rehired without discrimination. The Board scheduled elections with the understanding that the workers would vote by secret ballot for representatives, and those chosen by a majority would negotiate collective-bargaining agreements with the employers on wages, hours, and working conditions. If they failed to reach agreement on any of these issues, the parties involved would submit them to the NLB for final adjudication.

The Board's interpretation of Section 7a—that the principle of majority rule was to prevail in elections and negotiations—

ran counter to the Johnson-Richberg position. The Board felt that this was a logical approach to make collective bargaining effective. When thirty-six of the hosiery employers refused to sign collective-bargaining agreements after the union had won most of the elections in forty-five mills, the issue was submitted to the NLB. On September 27, the Board ruled that their action was in defiance of the "interest" of the earlier agreement, and that both parties had the responsibility of working out such "written agreements." The employers' subsequent compliance with the Board's recommendation signaled a major victory for the NLB's interpretation of Section 7a.

Shortly thereafter, the Board facilitated settlement of a silk strike in Paterson, New Jersey, and of auto strikes in Detroit. On October 16, it negotiated the end of a long stoppage by ten thousand workers against the company-dominated union at the Weirton Steel Company works in West Virginia and Ohio, along the lines of the Reading Formula. An election was scheduled for the second week in December to determine employee representatives. In late October, the captive-mines strike was similarly ended when the President used the Reading Formula to insure elections the latter part of November.

In the process of establishing a "common law" understanding of Section 7a, the NLB interpreted the language of the law—its statement that employees were to be able to organize and choose representatives "free from the interference, restraint, or coercion of employers . . . or their agents"—as prohibiting a number of discriminatory practices as well as the company-dominated union. The importance of this "common law" interpretation was that it survived the first NLB and became a precedent for its successors. The original NLB ruled that union membership could not be a cause for discharge, demotion, deprivation of seniority, or transference of work from an organized to a nonunion plant. Workers could, in elections, select "outside" individuals as spokesmen in negotiations; both strikers and non-strikers were eligible to vote in elections, but not individuals hired during the strike. Detailed provisions insured secrecy in voting and the validity of the election returns. Representatives elected by a majority of those voting bargained for all the workers in the unit.

Bernstein, *Turbulent Years,* 173–75, 176; Orme W. Phelps, "The Right to Organize: A Neglected Chapter in American Labor History," in Morton J. Frisch and Martin Diamond, eds., *The Thirties: A Reconsideration in the Light of the American Political Tradition* (DeKalb, Ill., 1968).

The National Labor Board in Retreat

As a result of the patience and determination of Wagner and the other Board members, along with the willingness of many employers and unions to cooperate during the initial enthusiasm for the NRA, the Board did a fairly effective job for the first three months. However, the absence of clear guidelines, and the receding crisis for management, enabled the hostile National Association of Manufacturers to launch a vigorous campaign against the NLB on November 1, claiming that its policies tended to "prevent the prompt and peaceful settlement of industrial disputes. . . ."

In two major setbacks in December, the first NLB was brought to its knees, and it never recovered. Ernest T. Weir defied the NLB when, over the vigorous protests of Wagner and the General, he conducted elections, at his three Weirton plants, only for company-union representatives. Although the Board subsequently requested the NRA to deprive Weirton of the Blue Eagle, no penalty was ever meted out to the company. The second decisive defeat involved the Edward G. Budd Manufacturing Company of Philadelphia, which refused to abide by a Board decision to end a strike and hold new employee elections.

On December 15, the President sought to save the tottering Board through an Executive Order which retroactively ratified its activities. But this was to no avail, for considerable portions of industry had, in effect, gone on strike against the NLB.

Toward the end of 1933, the Board was in serious difficulties, and Wagner's subsequent attempt at an optimistic appraisal failed to convince perceptive observers or alter the deteriorating situation. Wagner maintained that of the 1,818 disputes (involving just under a million workers) handled during its first six months by the NLB or its regional boards, 69 percent were settled. Another approach to these same figures, however, was to look at the "bona fide" settlements, those reached through satisfactory agreements or decisions undertaken by the NLB. According to this measuring rod, success was limited to 919 cases, which was closer to 50 percent than to Wagner's figure. But most significant was the declining trend in agreements. During its first three months, the NLB settled 104 of 155 cases, for a 67 percent result. By contrast, in the next three months it successfully arbitrated only 28 of 86 cases, or less than one-third.

These figures demonstrated that increasing numbers of employers were not only denying the jurisdiction of the NLB but ignoring its decisions. In addition, many disputes were not being settled satisfactorily because employers refused to concede the right of their employees to bargain collectively.

It was now clear to Wagner that both the NLB and the regional labor boards were without adequate enforcement authority. Their powers were not clearly defined, and could not be implemented to compel acceptance of Board decisions. The boards had too few competent investigators to pursue complaints seriously, and too few staff members who could apply the law objectively and facilitate speedy decisions. And they did not have the power to punish for contempt, or to subpoena witnesses. The result, too often, was interminable delays by Johnson, Richberg, and industry-trained spokesmen in the NRA in carrying a case up to the NLB. Time was of the essence in settling a controversy, but management, inspired by the NAM's campaign of opposition, now resorted to a variety of delaying tactics, aided by cohorts in the NRA and the NLB, to frustrate union endeavors. In the face of increasing defiance by

Budd Manufacturing, Weirton Steel, and industry spokesmen, Chairman Wagner decided that he had no alternative but to ask Congress to, at least, expand the powers of the National Labor Board.

Meanwhile, although FDR could inveigle a William Green to surrender fundamental rights accorded labor by the NIRA, as in the automobile code, the President failed, in private conference, to convince industrialist Weir to adhere to the NLB's interpretation of Section 7a. Despite the fact that the steel workers' union claimed to represent three-fourths of the twelve thousand employees of the Weirton Steel works, management continued to deny the NLB the right to supervise an independent poll of the workers. A frustrated Roosevelt soon directed that the Weirton Steel case be returned to the Department of Justice for adjudication in the courts. This was obviously one of the key test cases for Roosevelt and the NRA, but the case of a chicken dealer from New York reached the Supreme Court first.

New Republic, September 20, 1933, 153, March 14, 1934, 131; Exec. Order No. 6511, December 13, 1933; *New York Times,* November 2, December 8, 12, 14, 1933; FDR to Cummings and Johnson, January 16, 1934, Roosevelt Papers, OF 466; Fine, *The Automobile Under the Blue Eagle,* 151–54.

NRA versus NLB

On February 1, 1934, the President made another attempt to resuscitate the National Labor Board, through Executive Order No. 6580. This granted the Board authority to conduct representation elections, when requested by a "substantial number" of employees, seemed to endorse the principle of majority rule, and in response to the Weirton and Budd defiance of the NLB, instructed the Board to refer noncompliance cases to the NRA administrator. While union leaders and progressive spokesmen hailed this latest turn of events, Johnson and Richberg cut short their rejoicing within forty-eight hours, and made public a developing split between the NRA and the Board. Resenting the NLB's autonomy within the NRA structure, and seeking to reassure a hysterical management, the two NRA spokesmen issued a statement "interpreting" No. 6580. They reaffirmed their support for proportional representation, and then insisted that the Executive Order simply provided a method whereby a majority could designate representatives while minorities and individuals retained the right to bargain on their own behalf.

It was now labor's turn to howl. The General and Richberg had undercut the President's endeavor to strengthen the NLB, and unless repudiated by Roosevelt, their position would destroy NLB's "common law" principle of exclusive representation by the majority spokesmen. Until forbidden by an Executive Order, management could now bargain with company as well as independent unions, and thus controlled an effective weapon with which to restrict the AF of L. Roosevelt did not repudiate or rebuke his NRA spokesmen.

On March 1, 1934, the NLB firmly rejected the Johnson-Richberg interpretation and ruled that the union selected by a majority of the workers was to bargain collectively with management in negotiating an agreement for all the employees. Which principle would the President support?

Within days, the President sought to move the NLB off dead center by severing its link with the National Compliance Board of the NRA, making its findings final, and increasing its membership to expedite action. However, a new strike wave demonstrated that organized labor had lost faith in the NLB.

When four thousand workers declared a "holiday" in the plants of the Aluminum Company of America, the NLB wired the AF of L union in charge that the strike should be "called off at once so that the Pittsburgh Regional Labor Board will have opportunity to investigate the case." The aluminum workers retorted that the Pittsburgh board was merely a body of "superannuated politicians" and "honorary pallbearers." The "holiday" ended twelve days after it began, when the workers accepted an 11-percent wage increase, with the stipulation that union recognition and the checkoff of union dues be discussed at subsequent meetings.

In addition, the bungling of William H. Davis, National Compliance director, in excluding eight hundred strikers from voting in the Budd Manufacturing poll had intensified labor's disenchantment with NRA's mediation activities.

The NLB-NRA crisis came to a head in the automotive industry, in Detroit, forcing the President to intervene. Half-hearted AF of L endeavors to organize auto workers during the previous year had met with little success in most plants. On March 4, angry union members in the organized plants notified General Motors and Hudson that they would strike unless the companies recognized the AF of L union, reinstated men discharged for union activity, and granted a 20-percent wage increase. Without funds or experienced leadership with which to sustain an effective picket line, and conceding defeat in advance at the hands of the mammoth, united auto industry, organizer William Collins wired Roosevelt that same day urging a government-sponsored settlement as a face-saving device. The NLB responded the next day, at the President's request, and persuaded the union to postpone the strike so that hearings might be held. On March 14, the union presented to the NLB its demands for elections under the Reading Formula. The following day, General Motors' executive vice president, William S. Knudsen, advised the Board that his company refused to deal, or sign an agreement, with a labor organization and would not recognize the authority of the NLB to conduct elections at its plants. General Motors condescended to discuss complaints with individuals accompanied by their representatives, but that was all. After Hudson's spokesman said the same thing, the union decided to strike on March 21. The day before the strike deadline, Roosevelt personally intervened upon the request of Collins, and union representatives agreed to another delay.

Determined to avoid collective bargaining at any cost, even at the expense of a spreading strike, the tough auto industry, through its National Automobile Chamber of Commerce, argued from an obvious position of strength and conceded nothing to the union. It had formulated its own code the previous summer, and by March 1934 had made clear its view that Section 7a was a mistake and that it did not intend to adhere to it. Furthermore, the President realized that the auto industry was spearheading a business boomlet, and feared that an expanding strike might set it back. In the mediation proceedings between March 21 and 25, 1934, Roosevelt and Johnson met separately with industry and labor spokesmen; the former refused to sit at the same table with union representatives.

On March 25, the President announced a settlement, at the expense of the union and at the sacrifice of the NLB. It provided for a tripartite Automobile Labor Board (ALB), with one neutral, one labor, and one industry representative, divorced from the NLB but within the NRA administrative system, and "responsible to the President." The ALB was authorized to receive and adjudicate charges of discrimination for union activity. While a compromise was reached on the question of seniority in hiring and firing, the auto industry won completely on the interpretation of Section 7a. The President defied his own National Labor Board when he afforded legal sanction to company-dominated unions in the auto industry, and endorsed proportional representation as opposed to majority rule and exclusive representation. The automobile industry, with the aid of the White House, continued to be exempt from Section 7a and the Reading Formula.

Green and union spokesmen had surrendered vital rights to management, for the agreement undercut previous executive orders, and destroyed what was left of the National Labor Board. Instead of using the threat of a strike, which might paralyze the industry at the peak of its busy season, as a potentially compelling weapon, union leaders had listened to the "dulcet voice in the White House and yielded to the pressure of patriotism." These old-line labor leaders, mollified by a labor policy which seemed more enlightened than that of Hoover's New Era, and overjoyed at being able to walk through the portals of the White

House, were momentarily convinced by Roosevelt that the settlement inaugurated "a pioneer effort in human engineering." At this critical juncture, the AF of L had surrendered a key opportunity to gain a stronger foothold in the automobile industry. But worse still was the realization by other trade unionists that industry had gained a decisive advantage by opening the doors to the legalization of company unions. Not only had organized labor's drive for greater equality of bargaining power been nullified, but NLB decisions providing that majority spokesmen should bargain for all the workers in a company or plant unit had apparently been rendered useless. Auto management became the spearhead of the attack of heavy industry upon organized labor, with the help of Johnson, Richberg, and the President.

Exec. Order No. 6580, February 1, 1934; Bernstein, *New Deal Collective Bargaining Policy,* 57–62; Schlesinger, *The Coming of the New Deal,* 144–51; Rosenman, ed., *The Year of Crisis,* 318–19, 524–25; NRA News Release No. 3125, February 4, 1934; Bernstein, *Turbulent Years,* 181, 182–84; *New York Times,* March 4, 28, 1934; *New Republic,* March 28, 1934, 185; Perkins, *The Roosevelt I Knew,* 304; Fine, *The Automobile Under the Blue Eagle,* Ch. VI.

5

Section 7a: Labor's Magna Charta? Part II

〜〜〜〜〜〜〜〜〜〜〜〜〜〜〜〜〜〜〜〜〜〜〜〜〜〜〜〜〜〜〜

BY MARCH 1934, labor was on the retreat in the automotive and other key industries, and with the exception of the railroad unions, was making little headway with Congressional legislation. Across the Atlantic, where the Great Depression had ushered in a nightmare in Western Europe, each nation responded with regulations, controls, and planning intended to isolate and protect it from the unpredictable behavior of its neighbors.

In England, Prime Minister Ramsay MacDonald sacrificed a lifetime of identification with the Labor party program of nationalization and broader social-insurance coverage, to head a new, Conservative-dominated coalition cabinet which in many respects carried out a policy of economic nationalism—abandoning the gold standard, devaluating the pound, and curtailing free trade through a system of "imperial preferences." It adopted severe retrenchment measures, reduced the dole payments to the unemployed workers, and sought to balance the budget. But unemployment persisted until the eve of the Second World War, when the nation adopted military conscription and an expanded armament program.

The Great Depression reached France later because its economy was more evenly balanced between industry and agriculture.

The French government, characterized by instability, with four ministries in 1933, was led in the early years of the depression by rightists, who adhered to a policy of retrenchment and economy. Not until the height of the French depression, and the advent of the leftist Popular Front in 1936, did Socialist Léon Blum, the new premier, introduce the "French New Deal" of shorter work hours and collective bargaining. But Adolf Hitler and Benito Mussolini would not permit Europe to solve its domestic difficulties in peace and isolation.

Since Mussolini had established an Italian dictatorship in 1922, he had divided economic life into corporate sectors, each purportedly determining working conditions, wages, prices, and policies for a particular branch of industry. The government, however, remained the domineering force, and sought to counter the Great Depression with some large public works and a drive for economic self-sufficiency. When these efforts failed, Mussolini turned in 1935 to military and imperialist adventures abroad to ease his difficulties at home.

Germany appeared to suffer most from the worldwide depression. Faced with economic collapse and tremendous unemployment, the middle class lost faith in the postwar Weimar Republic, which had not had time to sink its democratic roots deeply into the fiber of the country. After the Hitler-led National Socialists had inflamed the public's fears of inflation, bolshevism, big labor, and Jewish capitalists, and throttled the Socialist, Communist, and labor movements, the Nazis gained power early in 1933. From that moment, Chancellor Hitler set about destroying organized labor; he forbade strikes, made bestial anti-Semitism an official policy, and absorbed the unemployed into extensive public-works, housing, and superhighway projects, and a vast rearmament program.

Back in Washington, D. C., Senator Wagner introduced his Labor Disputes Bill, S. 2926, in the Senate on March 1, 1934, and Representative Connery of Massachusetts offered an identical measure, H.R. 8423, to the House. Wagner maintained that the rights of workers to association and bargaining, as set forth by Section 7a, had collapsed in the face of management's restrictive practices, and particularly the promotion of company unions.

The Wagner-Connery bill was bitterly fought by most of the nation's newspapers, the Communist party, and the NAM, which mobilized trade associations, management, and company unions to testify, issue news releases, sponsor radio broadcasts, and exert unyielding pressure upon the White House. During extensive hearings by the Senate Committee on Education and Labor, in March and April, supporters included NLB representatives, the AF of L, government experts, the Socialist party, an ambivalent Secretary Perkins, and a less favorable, somewhat equivocal Johnson. Wagner's proposal sought to outlaw a number of "unfair labor practices"—the initiation and financing of company unions, interference with the selection of employee representatives, the refusal to recognize or deal with such representatives, and the failure to make every reasonable effort to make and maintain agreements governing wages, hours, and other conditions of labor. It also provided for a permanent national labor board to enforce its provisions, mediate labor disputes affecting interstate commerce, and through elections or otherwise, determine whom employees wished to have represent them in collective bargaining.

By the time the hearings were concluded on April 19, the President had decided to deny the Wagner bill his official endorsement. Committed to the NRA, which depended on business cooperation, the President was not prepared to battle big industry, now united in opposition to the bill. Also, the President's very recent concessions in the automobile settlement had alerted lawmakers to his opposition to any legislative move to strengthen workers' rights. And finally, members of a weary Congress, with considerable legislative achievement behind them, were anxious for a respite so that they could return home to mend fences before the fall elections. They did not want to become further involved, at this time, in exhausting debates which might take weeks to conclude.

Yet some adequate disputes machinery was necessary to cope with the waves of strikes which were threatening to engulf the country. Massive social upheavals in Toledo and Minneapolis would be followed by the San Francisco general strike in July, and a national textile strike in September. Labor unrest was general.

In May, Johnson and Roosevelt were suddenly confronted with a rank-and-file revolt, by steel workers, with many ramifications. Capturing control of the resolutions session of the national convention from the moribund, craft-oriented leadership of the Amalgamated Association of Iron, Steel and Tin Workers, militant spokesmen pushed through a motion demanding that employers enter into immediate negotiations with the union. If agreements were not reached by June 10, the union would call a nationwide steel strike six days later. The huge, well-organized, and richly endowed Iron and Steel Institute, the industry association, immediately welcomed and laid plans for this confrontation with labor. With a long tradition of bitter, anti-union hostility, steel management was most anxious for the opportunity to destroy the militant spokesmen as well as the union itself. This probable outcome was gradually recognized by many of the rank-and-file leaders, who then sought a way out of their dilemma. It was to be supplied by Roosevelt.

It seemed inevitable that if the reluctant, old-line union leadership was forced to carry out the convention's strike mandate, the nation's steel mills would be shut down in mid-June, the economy would be disrupted, and bloodshed would ensue. Faced with this prospect, the Chief Executive decided upon a new approach. With Republican support, he proposed a non-controversial enabling statute, to give him authority to create industry-wide mediation boards, whose powers would subsequently be defined by executive order.

On June 14, while a resolution to this effect was being developed, the President conferred with William Green in the White House. Although strongly committed to Wagner's labor-disputes bill, an unhappy AF of L chieftain agreed to support

Roosevelt's latest proposal, and to carry it to the special strike convention of steel workers the following day. There, disclosing the President's plans for impartial industry-wide boards to investigate and adjust complaints, to mediate and propose voluntary arbitration, and to hear cases of discrimination and discharge in violation of Section 7a, Green urged cancellation of the strike call. This new agency, he advised the convention, would have authority to supervise elections of worker representatives for collective bargaining under 7a, would have subpoena power, and could resort to the circuit courts for enforcement. Later that same day, after pro-strike militants had apparently spent too much time at the liquor bar, the convention rescinded the strike call.

In Washington, meanwhile, within a week after the President had planned strategy with Wagner, Perkins, Richberg, and Congressional Democratic leaders, and after accepting most of the amendments offered by Senate Republicans, the majority leaders submitted Roosevelt's proposal—Public Resolution No. 44—to both houses on June 15. The Seventy-third Congress was coming to an end, and everyone was anxious to adjourn. In the process of debate, however, progressive Republicans in the Senate expressed their unhappiness with the President's tactics, and stressed the need for a more comprehensive response, along the lines of the Wagner proposal, to the industrial strife sweeping the nation. Speaking for Norris, Nye, Cutting, and others, Wisconsin's La Follette moved to substitute Wagner's original bill, after denouncing the President's recommendation as "hasty and ill-considered." Only when Wagner pleaded with La Follette to support the President and allow the New Deal an additional period of trial and error, and after Wagner assured him that action on his bill would be certain in the next session of Congress, did La Follette reluctantly withdraw his amendment. An exasperated Bronson Cutting voiced the sentiments of many progressives when he blurted out, "The New Deal is being strangled in the house of its friends."

The joint resolution, which was railroaded through an un-

prepared lower chamber without a roll call the day after its
introduction, was adopted by the Senate twenty-four hours later
by a vote of 82 to 3. The House then approved the Senate's
amendments. On June 19, a day after Congress adjourned, the
President signed the bill. Ten days later, an Executive Order
abolished the NLB and created, under Public Resolution No. 44,
a three-person National Labor Relations Board (NLRB), nomi-
nally under the jurisdiction of the Labor Department. The NLRB
could investigate and mediate labor-management disputes, order
and hold elections, hear discharge and discrimination cases, act
as a voluntary arbiter, and issue regulations. It could recommend to the President the granting of additional authority to
existing boards.[1]

Industry appeared satisfied with the President's compromise,
while the old-line leadership of the AF of L, which had been
consistently loyal to Roosevelt, now felt bitter because of his
rejection of the original Wagner proposal. Both were correct in
their appraisals, for a close study of the joint resolution disclosed a major defect—its ambiguity. While giving the government an undefined power to intervene in any labor dispute and
to promulgate orders and regulations as desired, it failed to prohibit such unfair labor practices as threats, intimidation, and
coercion by employers. Its provision for government-supervised
elections was practically meaningless, for no obligation was imposed on employers to recognize the workers' representatives,
once chosen. Thus, the company-union issue was left precisely
where it stood before.

Equally significant for the future of the NRA was the role
played by Richberg during these developments. In a measure he
drafted for the NRA, Richberg proposed the elimination of many
of the pro-labor clauses of Wagner's original bill, and he then
helped circumvent that bill through the formulation of Public

1. The newly appointed members of the NLRB were Lloyd K. Garrison, dean of the University of Wisconsin Law School, as chairman;
Harry A. Millis, head of the University of Chicago Economics Department; and Edwin S. Smith, a Massachusetts labor-compliance officer.

Resolution No. 44. His support of the joint resolution pleased industry, but it did not clarify the confusion, which continued to surround Section 7a, about whether labor's collective-bargaining representatives were to be chosen by majority rule or proportional representation. His attitude toward Wagner's bill, following upon his undercutting of the President's efforts to strengthen the NLRB, and his vigorous support of Johnson and virtually every fundamental of NRA policy, now made it clear that Richberg had emerged as a principal conservative voice within the New Deal.

New York Times, March 28, May 27, June 13–15, 1934; Rosenman, ed., *Public Papers of FDR, III, The Advance of Recovery and Reform, 1934,* 300, 322–27; Bernstein, *New Deal Collective Bargaining Policy,* 72–75, 77, 82; Sen. Jt. Res. 143 and H.R. Jt. Res. 375 (73d Cong., 2d sess., June 13, 1934); Exec. Order No. 6763, June 29, 1934; Vadney, *The Wayward Liberal,* 130–35; *Congressional Record* (73d Cong., 2d sess.), LXXVIII, pt. XI, 4, 12017–12018, 12027–29, 12041, 12044, 12052, 12120–22, 12236–37, 12453; Bernstein, *Turbulent Years,* 197–205.

Johnson Violates Section 7a

Despite the separation of labor-mediation facilities from the NRA, Johnson soon provoked civil war between himself and organized labor. He achieved this through his personal involvement in at least three labor-management disputes (two of them of national scope)—the Donovan case in NRA headquarters, the longshoremen's strike on the West Coast, and the textile strike. In the process, he fell victim to Section 7a, and to the rapidly expanding forces seeking his removal.

Superficially, the case of John Donovan concerned discrimination against an employee because of his union-organizing endeavors. However, it had widespread ramifications for the future of organized labor inasmuch as it directly involved the NRA administrator, who was in ultimate charge of the NRA's compliance machinery and, therefore, entrusted with enforcement of its labor provisions.

According to the eventual findings of the National Labor Relations Board, Johnson had dismissed Donovan from the NRA Washington staff because of activities as president of its employees union. Shortly after the NRA local of the American Federation of Government Employees was formed in December 1933, Johnson conferred with Donovan and a union delegation on the subject of overtime work. One result was that immediate steps were taken to improve working conditions in NRA headquarters. Some six months later, while listening to Donovan protest the dismissal of another union member, Johnson insisted on speaking to him "as an employee," rather than as a union representative. After refusing to keep another appointment with Donovan, on June 18, or to grant him a subsequent one, the General summoned him to his office and fired him. Shortly thereafter, Johnson was given a severe jolt, and the nation some much-needed humor, when he was greeted by a picket line before NRA headquarters with banners proclaiming "Chiseler No. 1 Johnson," and "This Concern Is Unfair to Organized Labor."

The official reasons given for Donovan's dismissal were "inefficiency, insubordination, and absence from duty two days without leave." The only instance of insubordination presented by Johnson's lawyers at the NLRB hearings, which the General refused to attend, was the persistence of Donovan and a union delegation in seeking another appointment on June 18.

Within two months of Donovan's dismissal, the NLRB rebuked Johnson for "unjustified interference" in union organization, and held that he had violated Section 7a. The General was directed to reinstate Donovan immediately. There was little doubt that Johnson had been under tremendous emotional strain when he blurted out to Donovan, "You're fired." The damning indictments being hurled against him and the NRA by Darrow's National Recovery Review Board, the imminence of a nationwide steel strike, symbol of labor's revulsion against Johnson's mishandling of the auto and other codes, and the President's removal of mediation machinery from the NRA, were all indicators of a collapsing organization.

Unless halted, the General's conservative, anti-labor tendencies could severely handicap the work of the new NLRB, for the latter had to rely on Johnson's cooperation and the NRA compliance machinery to enforce its decisions. Since its creation in early July, the Garrison-led NLRB had taken Section 7a seriously and had cut through many administrative delays which had torpedoed the work of the earlier Board. However, in a number of cases referred to the NRA's Compliance Division for immediate removal of the Blue Eagle, if not prosecution, NRA headquarters had responded hesitantly, if at all. Somewhat typical was the case of the Chicago Motor Coach Company, which had been found guilty by the Chicago Regional Labor Board on April 5, 1934, of discharging employees for union activity. NRA headquarters had done nothing to implement the decision, except to return the case to the NLRB. After reviewing it on July 30, the NLRB immediately forwarded it to the NRA Compliance Division, insisting that "this Board will not be used as an instrument for destroying by delay the rights it was created to protect." Upon the General's orders, the NRA virtually ignored the findings of the NLRB and pursued an investigation of its own. Only after the Chicago Motor Coach workers went on strike was the NRA's Compliance Division catalyzed into recalling the company's Blue Eagle. The NLRB members now realized that they were confronted with some degree of sabotage by another New Deal agency.

New York Times, August 11, 22, 1934; William P. Mangold in *New Republic,* July 11, 1934, 237, September 5, 1934, 103–104.

Revolt in San Francisco?

Increasingly disenchanted by the roles of Johnson and Richberg, by the President's submission to management in the automobile "settlement," and by the inability of the New Deal to halt industry's disregard of the law, a million and a half working men and women in 1934 replied to recalcitrant employers with the only weapon left at their command, the strike.

Within days after Congress adjourned in mid-June, FDR officially intervened in the six-week-old strike of longshoremen on the Pacific Coast. Despite an overall lukewarm labor record, the New Deal administration appeared, in this instance, to be on the side of the striking workers. Aware that California's state and local governments, and most newspapers and civic bodies, were dominated by bitterly anti-union industrialists and financiers, and that there was a long and bloody history of labor-management warfare (symbolized by the imprisonment of union martyr Tom Mooney since 1916) FDR's staff labored for months to insure a peaceful settlement.

Fifteen years before, waterfront employers in San Francisco had taken advantage of the highly publicized, anti-union campaign with which business associations engulfed the nation after the First World War, to destroy a longshoremen's union during a violent strike. Management then gained absolute control over hiring through a new, company-oriented union and the "shape-up"—a hiring system which had been abandoned over forty years ago in the port of London, England. Other West Coast employers established hiring halls which they dominated, in Seattle in 1921 and in Portland and San Pedro in 1923.

Of some four thousand longshoremen in San Francisco, close to one thousand had regular work with steamship companies or stevedoring contractors. Their average monthly earnings in 1926 had ranged from $119 to $202. By 1933, the average monthly wage of longshoremen in San Pedro was a little over $40, and more than 50 percent were on relief. With industry in a serious decline after 1929, employers resorted to a killing speed-up which exhausted the strongest and led to many serious, if not fatal accidents. The thousands of casual workers suffered unbelievable treatment as victims of corruption and degradation from the moment they gathered, or shaped up, in the early morning hours near the Ferry Building at the foot of San Francisco's Market Street. They waited fearfully for hours along the cold, fog-enshrouded Embarcadero, which they called the "slave market," hoping that by eight o'clock, one of the foremen would hire them for the day. As Irving Bernstein interpreted the depressing picture years later:

Aside from slavery itself, it is difficult to conceive of a more in-human labor market mechanism than the shape-up. It brought out many more men than were needed, some of them social outcasts who neither would nor could take a steady job. It aggravated the inherent instability and insecurity of longshore labor. It assured the employer that he would not pay for idle time even when it was his fault. It freed him of restraint in increasing the tempo of work. More serious, it made a tyrant of the hiring foreman. . . . The longshoremen who worked on the Embarcadero detested it and awaited the day of its extinction.[2]

Shortly after enactment of the NIRA, a local of the International Longshoremen's Association (ILA) was revived in San Francisco under conservative union leadership. By October 1933, the ILA had grown in membership until it represented, for all practical purposes, the San Francisco longshoremen. While shipowners and stevedoring contractors sought to frustrate further ILA growth by a ten-cent-per-hour wage increase in December 1933, they refused to have anything to do with the union.

By the time the Pacific Coast ILA convention convened on February 25, 1934, the rank-and-file militant leader Harry Bridges was in command. An expatriate from Australia who had never secured his final citizenship papers, Bridges was an honest, incorruptible longshoreman who had worked closely with Communist trade unionists, expounded the Marxist dogma of the class struggle, and often parroted the party line. A man of inestimable courage and deep devotion to fellow workers, Bridges pushed through resolutions demanding replacement of the shape-up with the union hiring hall, a significant increase in hourly wage rates, a six-hour day, and a thirty-hour week. Unless these demands were met, the union would strike on March 23. George Creel, of the San Francisco Regional Labor Board, was hampered in his attempt to mediate a settlement

2. Bernstein, *Turbulent Years*, 255.

by the shipowners' refusal to make any concessions to labor in the formulation of an NRA code. They refused to discuss a change in the shape-up, denounced the union hiring hall as the closed shop, illegal, and in conflict with the Johnson-Richberg interpretation of Section 7a, and ridiculed the economic demands. By mid-March, virtually all Pacific Coast longshoremen endorsed the Bridges program. Like management in the automobile and steel industries, the shipowners—as they made clear to Creel—were prepared to lose millions and undergo a debilitating strike in order "to destroy the union."

On March 22, in response to a direct appeal from Roosevelt, the ILA postponed the strike pending investigation of the issues by a board composed of the chairmen of the three Pacific Coast Regional Labor Boards. After four days of hearings, the board recommended on April 1: representation elections under the Regional Labor Boards, the establishment of jointly controlled hiring halls in each port, and arbitration of wages and hours by another board.

Basing their response upon the President's automobile settlement of March 25, which endorsed the principle of proportional representation, the waterfront employers of San Francisco were willing to recognize the ILA as the majority—but not the exclusive—spokesman for the longshoremen and to set up a cooperatively controlled dispatching hall. No mention was made of wages. Standing firmly behind Bridges and their original demands, the longshoremen rejected this "settlement." On May 9, they went out on strike, closing down the entire coast. Within days, the longshore strike became a maritime strike as offshore unions threw in their lot with Bridges and the ILA.

The striking longshoremen quickly rejected the efforts of Assistant Labor Secretary Edward F. McGrady to establish negotiating committees empowered to enter into a final settlement. And after two endeavors by the national ILA president, Joseph P. Ryan, to sell them out to the shipowners, Pacific Coast longshoremen sent Ryan scurrying back to his more amenable, corrupt waterfront in New York.

By June 5, the strikers in San Francisco were confronted with new opposition leadership in the form of the Industrial Association, an organization of the city's leading industrial, banking, shipping, railroad, and utility interests. Since 1921, the Industrial Association had successfully deprived most of San Francisco labor of its collective-bargaining rights and all but insured an open-shop city. Its members were not about to surrender to Bridges and the ILA. The striking unions responded with formation of the Joint Marine Strike Committee, but it was no match for the amply funded, highly publicized endeavors of the politically powerful Association.

When San Francisco's Mayor Angelo Rossi was advised by the Industrial Association that it intended to reopen the port with strikebreaking truckers and warehousemen during the last days of June, a move which meant violence and bloodshed, he joined with California's Senator Hiram Johnson in appealing to Washington for aid. Acting under Public Resolution No. 44, adopted only days before, the President responded with an Executive Order creating the National Longshoremen's Board on June 26. To it he named Catholic Archbishop Edward J. Hanna of San Francisco as chairman, D. K. Cushing, a prominent local attorney, and Assistant Labor Secretary McGrady. They were to investigate the causes of the strike, and if authorized by the disputants, they were to arbitrate the controversy over control of hiring halls and the charges of discrimination for union activity.

On Tuesday, July 3, the Association hesitantly commenced truck haulage of cargo for the first time in almost two months. The inevitable happened when seven hundred armed policemen sought to break through picket lines along the Embarcadero. After four hours of fighting, in which police resorted to tear gas and bullets, twenty-five persons were hospitalized. But it was the events of "Bloody Thursday," July 5, the day the Association really resumed hauling cargo, that infuriated workers throughout the Bay area and catalyzed San Francisco labor into a general strike. As one reporter for the San Francisco

Chronicle put it, after witnessing running battles involving thousands of pickets and a heavily armed police force which had grown to eight hundred: "War in San Francisco. Blood ran red in the streets of San Francisco yesterday."

Innocent bystanders as well as strikers fell victim that day as tear gas and then bullets struck down scores of individuals. When the smoke finally cleared, two pickets were dead—a longshoreman and a culinary worker—and sixty-seven injured, some critically. No policeman was shot. That same afternoon, Governor Frank F. Merriam ordered five thousand National Guardsmen to take over the waterfront. With the industrial, financial, newspaper, and police powers lined up against them, and thousands of National Guardsmen with bayonets patrolling the Embarcadero, the striking longshoremen faced disaster. They were momentarily rescued, however, by the revulsion and anger which surged through the San Francisco Central Labor Council, which met within twenty-four hours, and by the decision of the local Teamsters and other key unions to join in sympathy strikes. The dramatic funeral procession on July 9, in which many thousands of sympathizers marched in silence up Market Street behind the two coffins, created a wave of sympathy which swept other unions along. Within a week of "Bloody Thursday," a partial general strike was in effect. Meanwhile, the Longshoremen's Board, holding hearings from July 9 to 11, was unable to move the disputants sufficiently. On Friday, July 13, the Central Labor Council voted overwhelmingly in favor of a general strike, and by the following Monday it was a reality.

The leading publishers of California, repelled by Roosevelt's New Deal and by former Socialist Upton Sinclair's EPIC (End Poverty in California) campaign for governor on the Democratic ticket, used their newspapers to lash out at the general strike as a Communist-led revolt against the nation. Uniting with Mayor Rossi, Governor Merriam, and the business and financial spokesmen of the state, they placed unyielding pressure upon conservative and moderate labor leaders. When

Governor Merriam voiced the sentiments of the Industrial Association and appealed to Roosevelt to rid the state of "communistic activities" through the deportation of aliens who had violated the law, he had Harry Bridges in mind. The hysterical governor of Oregon, Julius L. Meier, urged a vacationing President to send the Army to maintain the peace and to "delegate to General Johnson the power of your great office . . . to enforce settlement." Although Roosevelt rejected any thought of delegating presidential powers to Johnson, and Labor Secretary Perkins knew full well the hatred of California's publishers and business leaders for Roosevelt, for Sinclair, and for the labor movement, the General nevertheless jumped into the cauldron with two unsteady feet and helped dredge up the worst of human vices.

Madison, *American Labor Leaders,* Ch. XIV; Samuel Yellen, *American Labor Struggles* (New York, 1936), Ch. X; Perkins, *The Roosevelt I Knew,* 315–19; Francis B. Biddle, *In Brief Authority* (Garden City, N. Y., 1962), 296–307; Bernstein, *The Lean Years: A History of the American Worker, 1920–1933* (Boston, 1960), 16–17; Bernstein, *Turbulent Years,* 255, 262, 273, 287–89.

Exponent of Mob Violence

For days prior to his departure from Washington to fulfill speaking commitments in the Midwest and on the West Coast in July, rumors had been rife that the General was about to step down from the NRA. This possibility seemed on the verge of reality, especially in view of the latest indictments by Darrow's National Recovery Review Board, and previous actions by the President. In its third and final report, on June 28, Darrow's board concluded that the interests of the nation and of the consumer had been ignored by Johnson and the NRA, and that they had done nothing "to remove or even to restrain" monopolistic practices promoted by the codes. Thus, the NRA had become "not the foe but the adjunct of depression."

That same week, FDR conveyed his increasing disenchantment with the General in two decisive actions. On the one hand, he eliminated the NRA from any future role in the settlement of labor-management disputes when he created the "impartial" National Labor Relations Board. On the other, he transferred Richberg from his position as general counsel of the NRA to that of head of the new Industrial Emergency Committee, as well as executive director of the National Emergency Council, apparently to coordinate relief and public-works agencies with the NRA. Some astute Washington observers questioned whether the President was serious about giving increased responsibilities to Richberg, and concluded that this was merely another of FDR's impulsive moves which could not affect the basic situation. Others interpreted this latest decision as accelerating the decline of Johnson and the NRA. Furthermore, a recent Executive Order had accelerated changes in NRA policy by restoring competition in government bids, which meant tearing asunder Johnson's price-fixing policies. But the General remained.

Johnson was again in a poor physical and mental state, having recently come out of the hospital, after another drinking bout, for the third time in less than a year. Worn out and embittered, he ignored the urgings of friends to resign. Unfortunately, he was determined to go ahead with a job he could not do, and overwhelmed with problems he could not solve.

Key members of the White House staff, left behind in Washington to carry out administrative duties while FDR toured in the Caribbean and the Pacific, were worried by the General's state of health. In coded telegrams rushed to the President, Louis Howe and Marvin H. McIntyre expressed the feeling that Johnson's five scheduled speeches were "highly undesirable" and a "vacation [was] essential."

Despite urgings from the White House, Johnson objected to canceling appearances in Iowa and on the West Coast, especially at the University of California at Berkeley. While promising to take a two-week respite after these meetings, he assured the vacationing President that these four speeches would be on a "purely noncontroversial and constructive basis." The President overruled his staff's recommendation, and the result was disaster.

Johnson's remarks in Iowa were not disturbing, but his approach altered dramatically by the time he reached the Coast. In Portland, on the eve of the San Francisco general strike, he inserted an appeal for labor-management peace in his prepared remarks. After calling it madness for both sides not to sit down and negotiate, he suddenly let loose with a blast against labor's most effective weapon when he insisted that "strikes never got anything for anybody."

By the time the General arrived in San Francisco on Monday, July 16, accompanied by his secretary, Frances Robinson, some 130,000 workers had joined the general strike. Virtually everything was closed. The strike committee, however, had exempted milk and bakery deliveries, medical and hospital services, light and power facilities, newspapers, ferry crews, and nineteen restaurants. In contrast to the violence of the preceding weeks, there was no disturbance at any time during the general strike.

Johnson quickly installed himself at the Palace Hotel on Market Street, the strike headquarters of the California newspaper publishers. All that night and on into the early hours of Tuesday morning, Johnson was with these publishers, not with striking labor leaders. Despite his earlier commitment to the President to keep hands off, the General permitted the newspaper publishers to make him the focus of their headlines and of the unfolding strike drama.

Tuesday afternoon, with a strike settlement no closer at hand, the General journeyed across the waters of the Bay to the open-air Greek theater on the Berkeley campus. The publishers had insisted that the university authorities revoke their earlier cancellation of this meeting. There, with all of the prestige of the New Deal behind him, Johnson threw calmness and justice to the winds and appealed to the worst elements of the community. In remarks carried by radio to the entire Bay area, he conceded, at first, that the right to bargain collectively had not been "justly accorded" labor by the shipping industry, and that the latter's position was "extreme and unreasonable." Suddenly, however, he made one of his sharp turns, and picking up the theme that had been insistently repeated by Mayor Rossi, Governor Merriam, the Industrial Association, and the newspaper publishers, he blurted out, "But there is another and worse side to this story."

The "worse side," he explained, was that subversive or communistic elements had planned for, and gained control of, this general strike which was "a menace to government. It is civil war." This "ugly thing" was a blow at the flag of "our common country and it has got to stop." Seeking to divide the striking workers and their old-line conservative spokesmen from the militant leadership of Bridges, the General insisted that it was the duty of "responsible labor organization," of "patriotism," to "run these subversive influences out from its ranks like rats," if it was to retain the respect and support of the American people. ". . . insurrection against the common interest of the community," he insisted, was not a proper weapon and would not be tolerated for one moment by the American people. "If the Federal Government did not act, the people would act, and it would act to wipe out this subversive element as you clean off a chalk mark on a blackboard with a wet sponge. . . . It would be safer for a cotton-tail rabbit to slap a wildcat in the face than for this half of one percent of our population to try to strangle the rest of us into submission by any such means as this." [3]

Not a word about the inhuman shape-up or the debilitating speed-up. That same afternoon, as if timed to Johnson's hysterical appeal to mob rule, well-organized, vigilante groups suddenly roamed the streets of San Francisco. They invaded left-wing union offices and Communist newspaper offices and soup lines, breaking windows, smashing office equipment, and beating up union men. Although more than five thousand National Guardsmen patrolled the streets, not one vigilante was halted. Instead, according to newsmen, armed police squads, "mopping up" after the mob raids, arrested as "Communist," at least three hundred

3. *New York Times,* July 18, 1934.

of those who had been attacked. The charge leveled against them in court was vagrancy. Scores of injured workers who were able to escape the police network found their way to hospitals and medical offices for treatment of their wounds.

From New York came vigorous protest from Socialist leader Norman Thomas and the Reverend John Haynes Holmes for the American Civil Liberties Union. Tolerance of violence against workers, they wired Governor Merriam, constituted provocation of violence in return. The liberal conscience of the nation was speaking, but Johnson and the reactionary forces on the West Coast paid no heed.

Johnson, *The Blue Eagle,* 321–25; *New York Times,* July 9, 10, 16, 18, 1934; McIntyre for FDR, via Navy Code, July 9, 10, 1934, Roosevelt Papers, OF 466; Bernstein, *Turbulent Years,* 288–89, 291–92.

A Labor–New Deal Alliance Survives

By Tuesday evening, July 17, as earlier emotions began to cool and cracks appeared in the general strike, conservative, old-line labor leaders started to reaffirm their leadership. That night, the Central Labor Council voted 207 to 180 to seek arbitration, and appealed to Roosevelt to intervene. The following day, the Longshoremen's Board, through Johnson, asked the unions to call off the general strike and agree to arbitration. On Thursday, July 19, by the close vote of 191 to 174, the Central Labor Council acceded to the Board's request. Within days, longshoremen up and down the coast voted decisively to submit all issues to the Longshoremen's Board and to be bound by its decision. Shipping spokesmen reluctantly agreed to go along with arbitration. On July 27, union longshoremen in San Francisco started unloading ships for the first time since May 9.

In sharp contrast to the automobile settlement, the decision of the Longshoremen's Board constituted for labor and for Bridges a resounding victory. After holding hearings in four key ports in August and September, and receiving testimony and exhibits which totaled some three thousand pages, the Board on October 12, 1934, handed down its judgment, which was unanimous except for Cushing's dissent on wages.

The shape-up was destroyed, for longshoremen would be hired through halls "maintained and operated jointly," and the dispatcher would be selected by the union. Wages were raised significantly, the weekly work hours reduced to thirty, and the days to six, and there were provisions for overtime pay. Employers were given the right to introduce labor-saving devices, as long as they did not interfere with the safety or health of workers. During the rest of the year, somewhat similar benefits were awarded to allied unions. But collective bargaining was not yet firmly established in the West Coast shipping industry when the Longshoremen's Board went out of existence early in 1935.

This time, Roosevelt had not thrown his weight to the side of his enemies. Instead, throughout these critical weeks, he and Perkins had labored strenuously to avert industry's resort to the Communist issue to break the longshoremen's strike. San Francisco's waterfront employers and the Industrial Association had gone too far in goading labor with their defense of the feudal shape-up. In contrast to the auto workers in Detroit, San Francisco's longshoremen refused to surrender meekly to a forbidding coalition, or to a volatile Johnson. By flexing its muscles over a vital issue of humanity, and taking advantage of a rare general strike, the New Deal gained the leverage which enabled it to step into the picture at a crucial moment in defense of Section 7a. And even class-conscious Harry Bridges could not be too displeased with the ultimate results.

New York Times, July 17–19, 1934; Bernstein, *Turbulent Years,* 293–98.

The Textile Workers Rebel

Not every strike ended in victory for the union. During the summer of 1934, many of the nation's workers laid down their tools and joined picket lines, only to be met by police, National

Guardsmen, clubs, bayonets, tear gas, and bullets. When truckers went out on strike in Minneapolis, hundreds were brutally assaulted, or wounded by police fire. Tear gas routed pickets in Seattle, while in Kohler, Wisconsin, deputy police killed one striking worker and wounded twenty others. And so the story went, day after day. But the greatest tragedy occurred in the South.

After suffering years of unemployment, hunger, and management oppression, restless textile workers finally found a voice in their union. Delegates at the national convention of the United Textile Workers of America in mid-August, embittered by mass violations of the textile code in the South, overrode the advice of their leaders and voted a nationwide strike for September 1. These recent recruits to the trade-union movement had to remind their own officials that the established minimum wage, in too many instances, had become the virtual maximum, so that thousands of textile workers were earning less in 1934 than they had in 1932. But even the minimum was not enforced, for many workers earned as low as seven dollars instead of the legal twelve dollars weekly. Hours of work had been cut to eight per day, but in many mills this merely meant new, debilitating speed-up schedules and the introduction of the stretch-out system. Those exhausted by the new work schedules were indiscriminately fired. The NIRA had officially abolished child labor, but it was being eradicated before the advent of the New Deal because of the cheapness of adult labor. And many skilled workers had been discharged and reemployed as "learners"—one means of evading the minimum-wage clause.

Since its inception, the Cotton Textile National Industrial Relations Board, subsequently called the Bruere Board after its weakling chairman, had been flooded with complaints from workers and the UTWA. The Bruere Board merely forwarded them to George A. Sloan's Cotton-Textile Institute, which invariably concluded that there had been no violation of the code. The Board remained singularly ignorant of the stretch-out evil, and did absolutely nothing about violations of Section 7a. Cotton-textile employers systematically discriminated against union members—firing plant committeemen who sought arbitration for grievances, and discharging employees for joining the UTWA, for distributing a labor newspaper, or for talking to a union organizer. Company detectives, and the blacklist, were again in extensive use in the South.

In December 1933, with bulging inventories in the mill warehouses, Sloan's Cotton-Textile Institute, in its role as the code authority, convinced Johnson that machine hours should be reduced by 25 percent, from eighty to sixty per week. Inventories declined, but so did employment and weekly earnings. The restriction was removed early in 1934, but in May the code authority convinced Johnson that the 25 percent reduction in machine hours should be reimposed for June, July, and August. The result, overall, was a drop in official minimum wages from $12.00 to $9.00 in the South, and from $13.00 to $9.75 in the North.

Bitterness swept through the ranks of the workers, who flocked into the UTWA. Its most effective spokesman, Vice President Francis J. Gorman, threatened to call a general strike if the new restrictions were put into effect. Recognizing the new strength of the UTWA, NRA spokesmen on June 2 mediated a tenuous settlement, which provided for union representation on the stillborn Bruere Board, and an official study of wages and productivity. But the 25-percent reduction in machine hours remained. Sloan's subsequent refusal to sit at the same table with a UTWA representative facilitated the final collapse of the Bruere Board.

With other workers throughout the country laying down their tools as a last resort against exploiting, repressive employers, it was inevitable that Southern cotton-textile workers would do likewise. At the union convention on August 14, the delegates voted unanimously for an industry-wide strike, with Gorman as chairman of the emergency strike committee.

A reluctant NLRB, responding to pressure from Perkins and the White House, attempted to circumvent the hopeless Bruere Board and mediate the dispute, but it failed. Though the UTWA was willing to arbitrate, Sloan and the Cotton-Textile Institute refused outright; they welcomed the imminent strike as providing an opportunity for them to crush the union. It was a poor time for labor to shut down the factories, for the warehouses were crammed with surplus textiles. Most important, the Cotton-Textile Institute was well endowed with ample funds, seasoned leadership, and the willing cooperation of the vital forces of a feudal Southern society.

On August 23, in a last-minute endeavor to meet some of the genuine union grievances and ward off the threatened strike, the President issued an Executive Order reducing the weekly hours of 200,000 cotton-garment workers by 10 percent (from forty to thirty-six), and increasing wages by 10 percent. Within days, the affected manufacturers assailed the order as "unwarranted" and defied the President to carry it out.

The textile workers began laying down their tools on September 1. At a Labor Day rally of trade unionists, one of the most conservative vice presidents of the AF of L declared that organized labor was frustrated by the NRA, and that workers were becoming disillusioned by the reduced promises from Washington. Out on the West Coast, a loyal New Deal supporter in the United States Senate, Clarence C. Dill, urged an end to the Recovery Act.

From the start, the press was generally hostile. Typical was the *New York Times,* which denounced the strike as lawless and subversive, and the strike leaders as breakers of the law.

And what did the strikers want? Their four major objectives were a thirty-hour week, minimum wages ranging from thirteen dollars per week for unskilled workers to thirty dollars for the highly skilled, elimination of the stretch-out, and recognition of the union, with reinstatement of all workers who had been discriminated against because of union membership.

The strike had begun on Saturday of the Labor Day weekend. By Tuesday night it had spread up and down the East Coast, soon involving some 376,000 strikers in "the greatest single industrial conflict in the history of American organized labor." Taken aback by the tremendous response to the strike call, mill owners in turn replied with armed guards, machine-gun emplacements, and spies. The governors of Alabama, Mississippi, Georgia, and the Carolinas called out the National Guard, with additional thousands of special militia, in an endeavor to keep the struck mills open. Union organizers and sympathizers were run out of mill towns, some union officers were kidnapped, and union telegrams were intercepted by management representatives in Western Union offices. Sheriffs evicted striking families from company houses, while the Alabama relief administrator, who was an official of a United States Steel subsidiary, ordered relief automatically cut off for all strikers in the state.

After remarkable union successes during the first week of the strike, with "flying squadrons" closing down hundreds of mills throughout the South, management began to gain the upper hand. In Georgia, where Governor Eugene Talmadge declared martial law, strikers were forbidden to engage in perfectly legal strike activities and were arrested as "military prisoners." More than a hundred men and women strike leaders were interred in a military stockade "for the duration of the war." Nine strikers were killed in the South, and two youthful pickets in Rhode Island. Scores were wounded by bullet, bayonet, and baton. Company stores refused credit to striking workers, union headquarters were invaded and destroyed by company police, and mill pickets—including women and children—were assaulted by National Guard troops. And yet, strike defections were surprisingly few. In the end, however, the union leadership could not cope with the rising hunger of its members, nor overcome the neutralist, noncooperative stance of the timorous, old-line majority in the AF of L Executive Council. Except for Lewis, Dubinsky, and the United Hatters, the AF of L did not respond to Gorman's appeal for financial and organizational help. Nor could the UTWA alone resist the combined assault from industry, local and state authorities, and General Johnson.

On September 5, while the strike still had its initial momentum, Roosevelt appointed a three-man board of inquiry, in accordance with Public Resolution No. 44. This board, which would be available to conduct arbitration, was headed by the Lincolnesque governor of New Hampshire, John G. Winant, a Republican with New Deal sympathies. Three days later, in the face of increasingly effective management attacks, Gorman appealed to Roosevelt and the Winant board to arbitrate the dispute. Employer spokesmen, however, rejected the UTWA offer to arbitrate, insisting, for the record, that the union had resorted to mob violence and had called a strike "against the government, the National Industrial Recovery Act, the code system and constituted authority." Sloan advised Winant that the existing code authority, which he happened to control, could resolve all problems, and that there was no need for arbitration by any outside body. Clearly, the mill owners desired only one result, the utter destruction of the union. And they were well on their way to attaining that goal when the Winant board undertook serious deliberations in mid-September.

New Republic, September 19, 1934, 141, 142, 147–49, February 6, 1935, 346, 347; *New Yorker,* September 15, 1934, 37; *New York Times,* August 23, 27, 28, 30, September 1–3, 1934; Alexander Kendrick in *Nation,* August 29, 1934, 233; Margaret Marshall in *Nation,* September 19, 1934, 326–29; Bernstein, *Turbulent Years,* 298, 302–4, 307, 310; Bernard Bellush, *He Walked Alone, A Biography of John G. Winant* (The Hague, Netherlands, 1968), 104–6; Galambos, *Competition and Cooperation,* 243 63.

Johnson's Final Assault on Labor

As the strike approached its third week, Johnson appeared as the principal speaker, in New York's Carnegie Hall, before a capacity audience consisting of the chairmen and other representatives of some four hundred code authorities. In his opening remarks, the General veered away from the evening's topic, NRA reorganization. To the prolonged applause of the audience, which again underscored the pro-business bias of the NRA code authorities, Johnson lashed out at the textile strike and at the "infidelity" of the union leaders. Referring to the agreement that he had arranged between the United Textile Workers and the government on June 2, which had averted a threatened textile shutdown, he denounced the current strike as an "absolute violation of that understanding" and questioned the right of organized labor, in general, to be viewed as a "responsible instrumentality."

In a return to the red-baiting technique which had stained his Berkeley address, during the San Francisco general strike, the General suddenly denounced the national textile strike as being "political" in motivation, rather than an attempt to improve economic conditions. He accused Norman Thomas of having inspired the strike call at the special union convention in mid-August. Thomas, he insisted, "had no business" being at the convention, yet he and others had circulated among the delegates and assured them that "the government would feed the strikers." Johnson then added that his "heart weeps," not for the striking workers and their hungry families, but for George Sloan, who after overcoming all opposition in the textile industry to "concessions for labor" in the NRA code, must now "take the rap in the dissension between labor and management." [4]

Turning, finally, to the theme of the evening, the reorganization of the NRA, the General unjustifiably dragged in the name of Supreme Court Justice Louis D. Brandeis in support of his own views on the unwieldiness of the immense NRA organization and on its projected breakup into legislative, judicial, and executive segments. Brandeis, the renowned pro-labor advocate, had persistently warned against developing institutional giantism.

The end result of Johnson's harangue at Carnegie Hall was that he delighted those in management and industry, especially

4. *New York Times,* September 15, 1934.

textiles, and enraged almost everyone else. Wilsonian and New Deal Democrats, including the President, were appalled by his tasteless and unwarranted references to Justice Brandeis. AF of L vice president Matthew Woll, who spoke at the same meeting, voiced the reactions of organized labor when he denounced Johnson's "unwarrantable utterances and prejudiced intrusion into the textile situation," and his irresponsible decision to "laud the textile employers and bitterly denounce labor in general" at a meeting devoted to NRA reorganization.[5]

Asserting that the General had shown himself "the demagogic partisan of the mill owners," Norman Thomas blasted back at Johnson and reminded him that he, Thomas, had addressed the UTWA delegates at the union's invitation, and had "expressly told the convention that not even the friendliest outsider had a right to decide the momentous question of whether or not to strike." The Socialist leader had offered to raise relief funds for the strikers, for he knew that the local relief committees in the reactionary Democratic South would not feed strikers, regardless of the favorable intentions of the national Democratic administration in Washington.

In concluding a biting letter to Johnson, in which he insisted that the nationwide strike was the only means of enforcing improvement in the textile industry, Thomas warned the General that his Carnegie Hall remarks "invite and increase the suspicion that under your leadership NRA may degenerate into a quasi Fascist scheme for standardizing work and workers." [6]

Members of the Socialist party would normally have been flattered by Johnson's appraisal of the power and influence of their spokesman, but its divided factions were much too busy with an internecine conflict which was destroying what little was left of Eugene Debs' once-promising movement. And the textile workers, who had generally voted for Roosevelt in 1932, were surprised to learn from the NRA chieftain that they really had no major grievances. As a key figure in the government,

5. *Ibid.*
6. *Ibid.*, September 16, 1934.

which had evidently assumed the role of impartial arbiter through groups such as Winant's board, Johnson might have been expected to display a certain impartiality. Instead, he appeared blind to the injustice of his violent, provocative antilabor speech. When denouncing the strike leaders for breaking the June 2 agreement, he ignored the clause which had stated that it was "without prejudice to the right to strike." Furthermore, the General offered no appraisal of the effectiveness of the June 2 agreement, no recognition of continued industry-wide violations of code minima, of the prevalence of the stretch-out system, and of management's neglect of wage differentials—all prime abuses leading to the strike. The storm which immediately enveloped Johnson was not dispelled until his resignation was accepted ten days later.

On September 20, Governor Winant hurried unhappily to Hyde Park to submit his board's recommendations to a vacationing President. With their acceptance, Roosevelt affirmed a catastrophic defeat for the UTWA, and a disastrous setback for generations of textile workers, and for social progress in the South. Recognition was denied the union; wages remained unchanged, pending government studies at some future date; the stretch-out system was untouched; Section 7a problems would be referred to a new labor-relations board; and the re-employment of strikers was left up to the employers. Two days later, a disheartened strike committee surrendered.

Within the month, Sloan and his Cotton-Textile Institute gave ample evidence of their victory and determination when some three hundred mill owners refused to rehire any of the workers who had gone out on strike. The new Textile Labor Relations Board, which the President subsequently appointed, added to the defeat of the union. Devoting most of its time to handling complaints alleging management discrimination against former strikers, the new board handed down a typical decision in a case involving many employees of the Alexander Manufacturing Company of Georgia who had not been rehired. As pickets, they had kept the mill closed for a week, but "lost" the strike when the mill was reopened with the aid of a "light military guard" provided by Governor Eugene Talmadge. The board ruled that since the strike had been lost, the company was under no obligation to reinstate the strikers who had been replaced by strikebreakers. The company was not guilty of discrimination, because "the failure to reinstate the strikers to their former position, was not due to their union activities, but to the fact that others had been employed in their stead . . . and no work was available for them after the strike was called off." [7]

With decisions such as this, Sloan and the Cotton-Textile Institute had little to fear from the New Deal and Section 7a. Not many complaining workers got their jobs back. Writing from North Carolina toward the end of 1934, a perceptive reporter for Harry Hopkins described the workers as living "in terror of being penalized for joining unions; and the employers . . . in a state of mingled rage and fear against this imported monstrosity: organized labor." [8]

New York Times, June 3, September 15, 16, 1934; Mary W. Hillyer in *Nation,* October 10, 1934, 414; Jonathan Mitchell in *New Republic,* October 3, 1934, 203–4; Schlesinger, *The Coming of the New Deal,* 312–13; Perkins, *The Roosevelt I Knew,* 300; Lorwin and Wubnig, *Labor Relations Boards,* 415–27; Bernstein, *Turbulent Years,* 315; John G. Winant et al., Report of the Board of Inquiry, September 20, 1934, RG 9, 1817, National Archives; Textile Labor Relations Board, Decisions, September 26, 1934, to May 27, 1935, RG 9, National Archives; Galambos, *Competition and Cooperation,* 263–67.

7. *New Republic,* April 24, 1935, 297.
8. Bernstein, *Turbulent Years,* 315.

6

The General Retires

THE NATION'S VOTERS had traveled far within six months in altering their views toward the NRA. In September and October 1933, hundreds of thousands of men and women in towns, hamlets, and cities across the country, had paraded hopefully under the banner of the evangelistic Blue Eagle. By the beginning of 1934, however, it was clear that the NRA had become the "National Run-Around" for consumers, minorities, and labor, while affording industry unique opportunities for "cooperation" and price-fixing free of the threat of the antitrust acts.

A quick reading of the front page of the March 11 issue of the *New York Times* conveyed a picture of continued recovery in industry and of increases in consumer purchasing power. Readers learned about the "Biggest Rise in Store Sales in Fourteen Years," with department-store sales having risen "16 percent higher in February, 1934, over . . . February, 1933." The business section, however, carried a contrasting interpretation of the same figures. Dollar sales had been rising only because of a 25-percent advance in prices within the year; the actual amount of merchandise being moved was decreasing for the country as a whole.

New York Times, March 11, 1934.

Johnson's Reorganizations

Confronted with continuing disclosures of damaging evidence by the Consumers' Advisory Board, by the Research and Planning Division, and by public hearings on price grievances, and aware that Senators Borah, Nye, and others were attacking with increasingly explosive ammunition, Johnson sought, unsuccessfully, to quell a rising revolt. The General had hoped to appease labor leaders by recommending the adoption of shorter hours of work and increased wages by industrial leaders at their conference in early March 1934, but he failed dismally.

Using the podium of a meeting of the nation's retailers in late March, Johnson appealed to Congress to shun the scuttling of the NRA by a flank attack from what he indiscriminately called advocates of the "old order." He denied that small enterprises were being oppressed or that capital was favored over labor, and typically invited critics to join the staff of the Consumers' Advisory Board. Of course, he neglected to add that there were already many competent individuals on the consumer boards, and that their advice was either ignored or suppressed. For example, economist Paul Douglas of the University of Chicago had failed to create consumers' county councils throughout the country to channel complaints and suggestions to Washington, because Johnson refused to be moved in favor of the plan even by his own Consumers' Advisory Board. Despite informed protests, made in advance, the General had sanctioned faulty codes and unwarranted price increases, and permitted himself to be pushed into corners from which he was now obliged to plead with businessmen publicly, as well as privately, not to raise prices "for God's sake."

With staff morale at a low ebb, and the NRA on the verge of organizational collapse, Johnson announced successive administrative reorganizations which made it difficult, if not impossible, for even knowledgeable observers to keep abreast of the changes. Although they were obvious endeavors to correct mistakes, and to meet some of the charges hurled at the NRA for almost a year, Johnson tended to confuse the picture by carrying them out with the bombast and high-pressure methods which had become his trademark.

In March 1934, apparently responding to NRA critics who

constantly underscored the absence of any long-range policy making, Johnson issued Office Order No. 74, which provided for a Trade Practice Policy Board. However, on April 9, before any policy board could be established, Office Order 83 repudiated Office Order 74.

As a follow-up to the President's automobile settlement of March 25, 1934, which provided for the Automobile Labor Board, and seeking to expand his authority over collective bargaining, Johnson four days later issued a highly publicized administrative order for the creation of labor-adjustment boards in every codified industry. But this order remained a dead letter, and labor unrest continued. Hence, in the face of the threatened steel strike, the President found it necessary to push through Congress his own measure (Public Resolution No. 44) authorizing the creation of industry-wide mediation boards.

Within days, in an endeavor to reshape and revitalize his administrative system, Johnson resorted to a "whole reorganization" of the four divisions representing the NRA's major classification of American industries. Some confused Washington newsmen interpreted these latest changes as a forerunner of stricter code enforcement.

In late May, Johnson acknowledged the increasing pressure of external criticism by easing the regulation of the service industries. He also responded to criticism from his own Consumers' Advisory Board and the Research and Planning Division by creating a new, representative Policy Group with a single administrator for policy and three deputy administrators, assigned to trade practices, labor provisions, and code-authority administration. By June 7, 1934, this new Policy Group recommended, and Johnson issued, Office Memorandum 228, which turned out to be one of the NRA's most famous and controversial orders, exemplifying the dilemma and problems confronting Johnson and the NRA.

After months of study in response to the Field Day of Criticism, and attacks from the Federal Trade Commission, the Consumers' Advisory Board, the Research and Planning Division, and now the National Recovery Review Board, Johnson suddenly reaffirmed his faith in the competitive ideal when he advised the public that code price-fixing was abolished and price minimums would be set only in emergencies. "Covert combinations" for the fixing of prices were henceforth barred, with the antitrust laws apparently to be enforced against violators. Following twenty-four hours of tremendous uproar from industry, and threats of wholesale resignation by business-oriented staff members, the General ordered a retreat and issued a clarifying statement explaining that this new policy did "not affect codes already approved." To those who could see through the smoke of battle, Johnson's latest statement seemed to indicate that price-fixing would continue as part of 263 of the 459 codes then in existence.

It was now management's turn to claim victory over the Consumers' Advisory Board and the Research and Planning Division. Actually, however, a stalemate developed, for during the weeks and months which followed there ensued heightened conflict within the NRA over interpretation and implementation of Office Memorandum 228. The result was further deterioration of an organization that was already collapsing, along with Johnson's leadership.

The General continued to press for full speed ahead in the revamping of codes and in the remodeling of the NRA. He switched and shifted officials, set up new boards and commissions, released more confusing statements, and pushed on at a lively pace. But as one columnist had observed weeks earlier, "it mostly amounts to running in circles and getting nowhere. . . . the General never rids himself of the idea that he can put over his proposition simply by main force."

Lyon et al., *The National Recovery Administration,* 56–67, 284–85, 448, 677–78, 702–3, 716–40; *New York Times,* May 28, 29, June 8–10, 16, 22, 29, 30, 1934; Schlesinger, *The Coming of the New Deal,* 135; *Newsweek,* June 16, 1934, 25–26; Tugwell, *The Democratic Roosevelt,* 221, 326–28; Tugwell, "The Progressive

Tradition," *Western Political Quarterly,* III (September 1950), 392–93, 400–2, 405, 420; Hawley, *The New Deal and the Problem of Monopoly,* 97–103; *New Republic,* April 11, 1934, 240–41, June 27, 1934, 168–69.

New Attacks on the NRA

By the time these reorganization plans were announced, the NRA had clearly failed small industry and the consumer, and was retarding, rather than stimulating, recovery. While earlier journalistic attacks on the NRA had come primarily from conservative sources such as the Hearst press, the Chicago *Tribune* and the Chicago *Daily News,* pro-New Deal voices were now joining the rising criticism. Walter Lippmann, who had supported the NRA from its earliest days, finally concluded that the General was in grave danger of losing the war against industrial anarchy. The sensible thing was to concentrate on the steel code and a few other important codes, revising them to insure competition and a genuine system of collective bargaining. The great mass of minor codes, Lippmann felt, should be permitted to expire, except where an industry really needed a code, wished it, and meant to comply with the social ideals of the NRA.

Another attack came from individuals active in progressive and reform circles, some of the very groups which the President had been seeking to conciliate since his inaugural. In a joint statement, Oswald Garrison Villard, Paul U. Kellogg, John Dewey, Roger Baldwin, Dr. Franz Boas, Elmer Davis, Paul H. Douglas, Robert S. Lynd, Josephine Roche, Father John A. Ryan, and others did not say anything fundamentally new, but did convey a heightened sense of disaffection with the Roosevelt administration. The people, they felt, were still waiting for the New Deal to bring prosperity, but were beginning to realize that it could not. Except for some well-meaning reforms, the "Roosevelt Revolution" had turned out to be a newspaper phrase. The NRA had become the instrument of the Chamber of Commerce and the trade associations, and whatever good had evolved from this and other reform and relief measures had been vitiated by

Roosevelt's catering to industry and management. In essence, then, the New Deal was "a fraud and a sham in spite of its humanitarianism."

The acid test of the New Deal, they contended, "lies in its effect on the actual distribution of the wealth which the machine age creates but which we have yet to find the way to spread and use." The answer was to increase the earnings of workers, which could only be accomplished through strong, independent unions. But the NRA, they insisted, had "made no determined effort . . . to bring unionization and collective bargaining to a point where the codes can be enforced." The signers of this statement called for the banning of company-initiated, company-financed, or company-dominated unions, and of compulsory arbitration, and urged strengthening of the power of the President to compel recalcitrants like Weir and Budd to accept true collective bargaining.

Minimum-wage provisions, they believed, had to be overhauled to provide that basic minimum rates would rise automatically with the cost of living. And since no effective consumer organization existed, they urged the creation of an independent agency of government with a free hand to defend the consumers' stake in society. They also proposed that relief be taken off the inefficient emergency basis and be made a subject of permanent planning, and that Congress enact laws establishing nationwide unemployment insurance, old-age pensions, health insurance, and a hugely expanded housing program.

One value of this document was its reiteration of the extensive criticisms hurled by liberals and progressives against the NRA. Roosevelt had to heed this statement if he wanted to move in the direction in which many supporters of the New Deal originally thought it was going.

Walter Lippmann, "Today and Tomorrow," New York *Herald Tribune*, April 4, 19, 24, 1934; *New York Times,* May 20, 1934; Alfred M. Bingham and Selden Rodman, eds., *Challenge to the New Deal* (New York, 1934), 4; *New Republic,* May 30, 1934, 58–59.

Darrow's Board to the Barricades

The most highly publicized attack on the NRA was leveled by Clarence Darrow and the members of his National Recovery Review Board—William R. Neal, a North Carolina hosiery manufacturer; Fred P. Mann, a retail merchant from North Dakota; John F. Sinclair, a New York banker; Samuel C. Henry, head of a druggists' association; and William O. Thompson, Darrow's former law partner.

Upon the insistence of Darrow, Executive Order 6632 was issued on March 7, 1934, providing that the Review Board bring directly to the President, rather than to Johnson, the results of its investigation of monopolistic tendencies in the codes and of the impact of these codes on small business, and its recommendations for changes. By this maneuver, the President sought to placate the increasingly vocal spokesmen of small business and to head off a full-scale Congressional investigation. Because of their controversial nature, the three reports issued by the Review Board's majority during the next few months had nationwide reverberations and accelerated the decline of the NRA and its administrator. Still vibrant and youthful despite his seventy-seven years, Darrow had been a well-known defender of labor and of the underprivileged since the days of the Pullman strike and of the trial of Eugene Debs in 1894. Now he presided over more than five weeks of intensive hearings to ascertain whether the NRA codes promoted monopolies and oppressed small-business enterprises.

At twelve lengthy hearings, beginning on March 15, 113 witnesses presented 2,753 pages of complaints concerning eighteen codes. When these initial hearings ended, 304 complainants were still awaiting an opportunity to testify concerning 104 additional codes. Since the President had directed that the first report be in his hands in little more than a month, it was almost inevitable that this document would be hasty and incomplete. Furthermore, the Review Board lacked the power to subpoena witnesses. Since it could not command both sides to appear, much of the testimony necessary for a complete appraisal was not available, and the investigation was restricted and to an extent one-sided—confined to the views of the complainant. Another shortcoming was the absence of a staff of experts in code law and economic research; they could have been of inestimable aid in digesting and translating the great masses of testimony that had previously been presented before various NRA and Federal Trade Commission hearings.

Perhaps in part for this reason, all three of the reports eventually presented to the President suffered from an almost complete lack of detailed statistical and accounting information. In the first report, for example, in citing the shortcomings of the steel code, the majority neglected to specify exactly how the code had affected the cost of steel production and the prices charged. No answers were offered for such vital questions as whether the code had widened the profit margin and encouraged profiteering. And if other codes were better than the steel code, what figures showed them to be better?

As a matter of fact, these same statistical and accounting shortcomings had helped doom the industrial-recovery program itself from the start. Without detailed knowledge concerning the actual costs and profits in individual companies, Johnson's NRA could not develop and enforce responsible codes. Experience had demonstrated that the costing systems introduced by private industry since the birth of NRA codes were designed to provide a basis for raising prices; they turned out to be "virtually useless for a price policy seeking the general welfare by enlarged output."

The inadequacies of the Review Board led to the early resignation of its vice chairman, John F. Sinclair, the author of the minority statement in the first report. In this statement Sinclair attacked his colleagues for approaching the investigation without "careful research and analysis." He felt that the majority conclusions very largely gave only one side of the situation and therefore were "inconclusive, incomplete and at times misleading and unreliable."

Sinclair did nevertheless agree with many of the majority conclusions, though he expressed his views in less colorful language, and without a comparable indictment of American capitalism. Much of the testimony had dealt with the difficulties suffered by the small businessman under the various codes. The main objection seemed to have been that in the process of working out the principle of self-government in industry, the small, independent businessman was largely ignored, both in the writing of the codes and in the designation of committees to enforce them. Many big-business leaders had early accepted positions in the NRA, supervised the writing of codes, and subsequently resigned; often they were then appointed to the code authorities, to administer and enforce the codes they had formulated. The result was that small independent businessmen were left without influence on the control exercised by the code authorities. Even the General had conceded to NRA critics in February 1934 that "the certainty of protection against monopoly control, and oppression of small enterprise, and, especially, the inclusion in codes of adequate buying (as well as selling) provisions to guard against oppression of small business is badly needed."

It was, ironically, the minority statement that spotlighted a damaging study on price-control devices in NRA codes by George Terborgh of the Brookings Institution. This study concluded that because of the original delay in the development of the codes and the speculative anticipation of their effects, prices generally rose before wage rates. And when wages were raised by the codes, the gain proved to be only about equivalent to the increase in the cost of living. The codes, therefore, did little to change the distribution of the nation's aggregate income. Terborgh's general conclusion was that the NRA had retarded recovery and had not insured the stabilization of business at the level of full production and full employment.[1]

Conceding that at least 20 percent of the complaints re-

1. George Terborgh, *Price Control Devices in NRA Codes* (Washington, D. C., 1934), 1; Lyon et al., *The National Recovery Administration,* 845–46, 850, 852–53, 859, 873–74.

ceived by Darrow's Review Board were "fundamental and important," Sinclair concluded that many a smaller businessman feared to report his real troubles to his code authority because its members were the most powerful competitors of the small independent within the particular industry. It was clear to Sinclair that many of the codes, embracing over 90 percent of the industrial payrolls of the nation, had been hastily drawn and should be amended "in order to protect the little businessmen from exploitation and monopoly."

The first report of 155 pages, completed in April by the other five members of the Review Board, provided support for the implication, found also in the minority statement, that there were irreconcilable differences between the actual workings of the NRA codes and the social, economic, and political philosophy underlying the Recovery Act. The majority contended that the government had sanctioned monopolistic practices and that some code authorities had administered codes for the benefit of the "big fellows." Many code practices had hastened "the exit of the small enterprises," fostered "the always growing autocracy of the greater," and deprived numerous wholesale purchasers of the opportunity to buy at lower prices from the factories closest at hand. If a number of recommended changes were not made quickly in the motion-picture industry, for example, small independent theater owners and operators would either be forced out of business or be dominated and controlled by the large producers, distributors, and affiliated theater owners.

A five-page "Special and Supplementary Report" by Darrow and Thompson engendered the greatest anger in the Roosevelt administration, for it not only pinpointed the dangers of monopoly inherent in the NRA, but contended that these practices would not be disclosed to the public "if fact-finding and enforcement are thus controlled by industrial combinations." To permit the NRA to carry out these obligations was to "expect violators of law to sit in judgment upon and to condemn themselves."

Darrow and Thompson insisted that only through the fullest use of productive capacity to raise the standard of living could an equitable balance be achieved in an age of abundance. And this could only be done "when industry produces for use and not for profit."

Johnson, *The Blue Eagle,* 271–76; report submitted to FDR by John F. Sinclair, member, National Recovery Review Board, April 14, 1934, Roosevelt Papers, OF 466; *New York Times,* February 28, May 3, 5, 8, 10, 12, 21–24, 1934; Lyon et al., *The National Recovery Administration,* 871–77; the Review Board's report on the steel industry was largely based on the Federal Trade Commission's recent report to the Senate on the iron and steel code (73d Cong., Sen. Doc. 159); National Recovery Review Board, *First Report to the President of the United States* (Washington, D. C., n.d.) mimeographed, 11–17, 33–48, 77–78, 80–81, 82–113, 125–27, 130–31, 133–36; Special and Supplementary Report to the President by Clarence Darrow, chairman, and William O. Thompson, member, National Recovery Review Board, May 3, 1934, 2–5, Roosevelt Papers, OF 466.

The General and Richberg Counterattack

For almost a month thereafter, the Review Board majority seethed in anger as the President refused to release the report to the public. Roosevelt insisted on giving Johnson and Richberg ample time to collate item-by-item replies made by the divisional administrators. When the collective results were released to the press on May 20, they were contained in five documents comprising some 150,000 words. And they set off one of the bitterest public exchanges of official correspondence in years, moving one observer to comment, "None of the reporting officials was inhibited in his effort to uphold his viewpoint and to offset, neutralize and discredit that of his opponent."

According to the General, a "more superficial, intemperate and inaccurate" document had never been issued. The Review Board majority had not acted in good faith, he claimed, for "after a few hours of cavalier inquiry and prejudiced and one sided testimony," it had presumed to pass judgment on codes which had required days and weeks of negotiation. Instead of offering fair and constructive criticism, the Review Board had acted as a political sounding board because of fixed prejudices, partisanship, and unfair methods of taking and reporting testimony.

Richberg's seventeen-page commentary bristled with invectives and caustic remarks hurled against his former friend Darrow. The report, he declared, was "a haphazard, one-sided investigation," one which sought to justify a preconceived opposition to the fundamental theories and purposes of the NRA. Further, he accused Darrow of pettiness, of making an unfair attack on another government agency, and of supplying "ammunition for the malicious sniping of political partisans, . . . of monopolists and . . . of chiselers. . . ."

The overall effect of this vituperative exchange was to create deep resentment and hostility within the NRA, to draw for the world at large a picture of an unmanageable administrative organization, and to exacerbate the very confusion which the Review Board had originally been assigned to clarify. The explosions which followed shook the Administration.

In the Senate, Nye denounced the "military arrogance" of Johnson and urged a complete and immediate housecleaning. On the Democratic side, hardly a voice was heard in defense of the General, Richberg, or the NRA. Only the majority leader, Robinson of Arkansas, had some kind words for the NRA administrator, and even he spoke with an obvious lack of conviction. The public debate and diatribes which subsequently flowed between Darrow, Johnson, and Richberg were shameful. Most Washington observers concluded that it was only a matter of time before the General was relieved of his responsibilities, for he had become too much of a liability to the Roosevelt administration.

In the midst of this raging public debate, in which Johnson characterized the NRA as "the greatest forward social movement of our day and age," and portrayed Darrow and other

opponents as "scribes," "Pharisees," and "demagogues," the
President took some hesitant steps in response to public clamor
and the Review Board recommendations. His first move was
to end the regulation of service industries, retaining only those
rules relating to labor's right to organize and to bargain collectively. He then created a three-member Appeals Board for
the sole purpose of protecting small business. Not long afterward, the General exempted shops in towns with populations
of less than 2,500 from most NRA rules, the exceptions being
the ban on child labor and the provision for collective bargaining.

The subsequent reports of the Review Board engendered
far less public discussion, but heated debate continued between
the principals. The second report, submitted on June 8, confined itself to the study of fourteen coded industries, with a
minimum of general comment. However, in an overall appraisal
of the administration of the NRA, it characterized the General
as a "dictator." William O. Thompson refused to approve this
report and then became the second member to resign. The Blue
Eagle, he insisted, had turned the little businessmen over to the
mercies of the trade associations.

Johnson's reaction to the second report was that it was
even "more inaccurate and inconsequential than the first." The
General insisted that after three months of "suppression of all
favorable testimony," and refusal to permit NRA spokesmen
the opportunity to defend themselves, the Review Board had
not been able to produce any "evidence that there is any monopoly or oppression at all." In fifty pages of detailed replies,
Richberg became more reckless as he denounced the Review
Board's "fevered criticisms" and its practice of "avoiding any
restrained judicial comment."

In its third and final report of June 28, 1934, the Review
Board observed that nothing had been done by the General or
Richberg "to remove or even to restrain" any of the monopolistic behavior it had previously uncovered. The NRA had
fostered and fortified practices under which 1 percent of the

nation's population possessed 60 percent of the nation's wealth. In this respect, the NRA had become the ally, not the foe, of the Great Depression. Further, by suspending the antitrust laws it had strengthened business combinations which tended toward monopoly, and it had supplied big businesses with the means "to silence, suppress, eliminate or ignore their complaining small competitors." Since "democracy must apply to industry no less than to politics," the Review Board maintained, every member of an industry subject to a code had to be guaranteed a voice in the election of the governing body, the code authority.

Finally, while commending the NRA for seeking to abolish child labor, shorten the hours of work, and guarantee to labor the right to bargain collectively, the Board concluded that the codes were too drastic and attempted too much. It had been a grave error to "deliver industry into the hands of its greatest and most ruthless units when the protection of the anti-trust laws had been withdrawn," for monopolistic tendencies had been strengthened through the "perversion of an act excellently intended to restore prosperity and promote the general welfare."

It was rather ironic that on the very day that the Review Board's final report was released, the annual conference of the National Association for the Advancement of Colored People condemned the NRA for its negative, if not destructive, impact upon black workers. A serious shortcoming of the Review Board was its complete neglect of the plight of minority workers. Indeed, the continued public, labor, and newspaper disinterest in ethnic questions was symbolized by the fact that the Review Board's indictment of the NRA was generally placed on the front pages, while that of the NAACP was to be found in an abbreviated version on page 13 of the *New York Times*.

Johnson to FDR, May 15, June 26, 1934, Roosevelt Papers, OF 466; commentary on the majority report of National Recovery Review Board—by Donald R. Richberg, general counsel NRA—summarizing the detailed analyses made by deputy administrators of the findings and recommendations of the Review Board concerning various codes, May 15, 1934, 3–5, 18, 19, Roosevelt Papers, OF 466; *New York Times,* May 28, June 1, 14, July 2, 15, August 8, 1934; Darrow to FDR, Roosevelt Papers, OF 466-E; National Recovery Review Board, *Third Report to the President of the United States* (Washington, D. C., June 28, 1934), mimeographed, 29–35; Raymond Wolters, "Section 7a and the Black Worker," 460, 464, 465, 469, 472.

The General Refuses to Surrender

Despite the highly publicized, critical report issued by the Darrow Review Board, and the continued setbacks inflicted upon blacks and other ethnic minorities by the NRA, Roosevelt continued to have the warm support of the bulk of the American people. This was especially true when voters faced up to the alternatives offered by the Republicans. When Congress adjourned on June 18, 1934, the lawmakers had granted the President complete power to revise the tariff, and had given him the Stock Exchange Act, the Communications Act, and the extension of the AAA, among other legislative enactments. By the summer of 1934, the Chief Executive had bypassed Lewis W. Douglas and those committed to balancing the budget, and had again become a convert to the policy of spending government money as the best and most effective means of increasing consumer purchasing power, stimulating business, and promoting recovery. He could no longer fall back upon the NRA to ease acute distress, because it had failed dismally. Labor had not continued to make gains, and recovery was stalled again, for industrial prices seemed far out of line with wages and farm incomes.

And yet, according to many signs, FDR was more popular than he had been in November 1932. The vote which had elected him President had been negative—against Hoover—but now the support he received was positive, and the recession of 1934 was not as detrimental to his popularity as might have been expected, for the economic downturn was from a peak considerably above that of November 1932.

When FDR visited Portland, Oregon, in August 1934, on his way to dedicate a nearby dam, thousands of men and women jammed the streets to bid him welcome. Even workers on strike, and the unemployed who lined the route, seemed to have hope reinstilled by the mere presence of the President. A knowledgeable, independent-minded reporter, who would one day represent Oregon in the United States Senate, commented, "All along the tedious drive through the mountain and wheat country, the story is the same. The people worship him. He is their idol." This same newsman reflected sadly on the fact that FDR, who could have done so much for them, had in reality done so little.

In a radio address to the public, after Congress adjourned, FDR asked the citizens to judge the nation's recovery by the effect on their daily lives. He suggested that they "Go back a year," and recall the situation. Roosevelt spoke of hundreds of thousands reemployed, but said not a word about some eleven million still without work.

At the fourteenth meeting of the National Emergency Council, in August 1934, Richberg reported a number of what he perceived as favorable indices, such as a significant decline in business failures, and an overall increase in employment as well as wages since June 1933. He ascribed this improvement to the President's Reemployment Agreement, the shortening of hours, and the establishment of minimum wages under NRA codes. However, along with this impressive array of figures, came Richberg's admission that the increase in per capita earnings—the rise in hourly compensation and in weekly earnings—had just about equaled the rise in the cost of living. Therefore, Richberg concluded, the average worker "is not better off in his individual standing, but there are more people employed."

At the twenty-fourth meeting of the NEC, the following February, Richberg reported that while there had been a 10-percent increase in income since the low point of 1933, not all groups of consumers had fared equally well. The greatest improvement had been among the unemployed, the lowest-paid wage earners, and the agricultural population. With public works and work-spreading under the NRA, there had been an increase in employment since March 1933 of about four million. But the estimated number of unemployed had still not fallen below eleven million.

Soon to be available to Richberg and the NEC members were vital figures from the Bureau of Labor Statistics (BLS), the census, and other business and industrial surveys. They would demonstrate that the NRA had been only partly successful in stimulating the reemployment of workers by a general reduction of the hours of labor. The number of wage earners in manufacturing, which in 1934 was 75.1 percent of the comparable 1929 total, was barely altered by May of 1935 to 77.5 percent. Although an NIRA objective was increased consumer purchasing power, BLS figures indicated that weekly payrolls in all manufacturing industries in 1934 had reached only 56.7 percent of the 1929 figures.

Between June 1933 and May 1935 the cost of living, according to the National Industrial Conference Board, increased by 13.8 percent, while in manufacturing, average hourly wages rose by 36 percent and average weekly wages by 18.5 percent. The failure of weekly and annual wages to keep pace with hourly rates in the automobile industry, the textile industry, and others, so far as comparisons with 1929 are concerned, is partly explained by the shorter hours and the more irregular employment of the NRA years.

Meanwhile, reports filtering through from the Commerce Building conveyed a picture of confusion reigning supreme within the NRA. There seemed no way of making it orderly and functioning. Adding to the chaos was the continuing lack of certainty about the goal toward which the President was heading, and how he expected to reach it.

Up to the day Congress adjourned in June 1934, extensive Senate hostility toward the NRA continued unabated. No one seemed impressed by any of the attempted reorganizations, or by various proposals to revamp the codes. Senators Borah and Nye continued to insist that the best course of action would be to remove the General. But despite hints and rumors, Johnson had no thought of departing. In fact, he was so unrealistic that in May 1934, he set wheels in motion to enhance his personal power dramatically. He requested FDR to transfer to him, as administrator for industrial recovery, the powers vested in the Chief Executive by Section 10 of the NIRA: to make all rules and regulations necessary to carry out the purposes of the Act, unless otherwise delegated, and to cancel or modify any code, rule, license, or order issued under Title I.

The furor which this request engendered in the inner cabinet should have facilitated the speedy removal of Johnson. Instead, the President took the easy way out by simply rejecting Johnson's proposal.

Richard L. Neuberger in *New Republic*, August 22, 1934, 44, 45; Seligman and Cornwell, eds., *New Deal Mosaic*, 274–75, 445; Fine, *The Automobile Under the Blue Eagle*, 121, 124–25; Cummings to FDR, May 24, 1934, and Perkins to FDR, June 18, 1934, Roosevelt Papers, OF 466.

The Final Retreat

Richberg persisted in his public defense of the NRA. By late June, however, even he advised the President that Johnson lacked the fundamental wisdom, and the physical and mental stability, to carry on as administrator. The General's recurring breakdowns and loss of control had seriously disrupted the functioning of the organization. And his condition was getting worse. In a two-page, handwritten draft, Richberg recommended that the General be required to "take a *complete rest* for 30 to 60 days," and that Johnson "*himself* appoint from NRA a Board of three (acceptable to the President) to serve as the Acting Board of Administration in his absence (Leon C. Marshall, Clay Williams and Blackwell Smith would be an absolutely competent board.)." Richberg then suggested that FDR suspend the functioning of the National Emergency Council for ninety days, transfer part of its duties to a newly created industrial council composed of three Cabinet members and two top administrators, and appoint him its director.

In an endeavor to calm Richberg, and to strengthen the NRA by circumventing Johnson, Roosevelt incorporated most of Richberg's proposals in an Executive Order in late June. A new Industrial Emergency Committee was created, and Richberg was appointed its director as well as executive director of the National Emergency Council. Theoretically, these new assignments would enable Richberg to coordinate all New Deal recovery activities. In reality, the changes were just another of Roosevelt's fast job shuffles which meant little in the long run.

As rumors spread of the General's breakdowns, and of the imminent collapse of the NRA, the President convened an emergency meeting of Johnson, Richberg, and Perkins at the White House on August 20. There, FDR sought to convince the General to take an extended leave, if not resign. A little earlier, Johnson had sent the President a four-page document in which he carefully charted the orderly transition of the NRA to its "second phase," that of supervising the organization of industries for self-government. Johnson made it clear that the time had come to replace him with something akin to a board of directors responsible for NRA policy and administration. The General felt that the "task of pioneering this great experiment is about over and . . . a different form of organization and method is more appropriate for the future problem."

However, when the President finally got around to suggesting to Johnson that he needed a rest and that he might undertake a study of European recovery programs, the General exploded and walked out of the White House. Later that same evening, Roosevelt received a three-page typewritten letter of resignation from an embittered Johnson, who then hurried back to his beach retreat in Delaware. Although Johnson's removal was long overdue, Roosevelt's reluctance to face up to the inevitable decision insured another apparent victory for the General. The President rejected his resignation, for the moment. News of these developments was leaked to the press by the General's forceful secretary,

"Robbie," who was determined that her boss either break with the Chief Executive in a dramatic exit, or be continued in supreme command. As far as the White House was concerned, the entire fracas was developing into an unfortunate public cleansing of dirty linen.

By the start of the national textile strike on September 1, the situation looked so bad to Richberg that he appealed directly to the President for immediate action to establish responsible control and to check the internal disintegration of NRA. When Roosevelt did not respond decisively, Richberg sent an additional memorandum indicating that things had become so desperate that delay in decisive action would be harmful to the Administration.

Not one of the four key men in the NRA desired to continue under the General's leadership.[2] Averell Harriman no longer found it possible to persuade useful men to join the NRA. The administrative divisions had become hotbeds of petty politics, jealousies, and fears, which negated any hope of reasonable efficiency. Conceding the validity of many of the criticisms which had been hurled at the General by Borah, Nye, and others, Richberg concluded that only his immediate removal could save the NRA. "A team of horses can't be driven in harness with a wild bull. That sort of cooperation is impossible."

Embarrassed by this latest turn of events, the President turned to Tugwell for a sampling of the opinions of his official family. Tugwell warned the President that the situation had deteriorated to such an extent that it could no longer be tolerated. Henry Wallace believed that a break with Johnson should be presented as arising from a personal question rather than from differences in policy. He urged Roosevelt to avoid making Johnson a martyr and the darling of big business. The General's sec-

---

2. The four key men, according to Richberg, were Colonel George Lynch, administrative officer; Blackwell Smith, assistant administrator for policy and chief of the Legal Division; Leon Henderson, head of the Economic Division; and A. R. Glancy, head of Compliance and Field Administration.

retary had already sought to influence the press to portray him as the defender of industrial self-government and freedom of enterprise against "political regimentation and socialistic control."

Virtually no one in government felt able to work any longer with the General, or regarded him as contributing effectively to the Administration. Thus, according to Harry Hopkins, at least 145 of the President's 150 highest officials believed that Johnson's usefulness had come to an end, and that he should be permitted to retire. If Johnson remained, it was felt, no matter what conditions the President might impose, the General would proceed, as he had in the past, to do exactly as he pleased by his usual devious methods.

The pressure finally built up to the bursting point. Wherever he turned, the General found people alienated and hostile. In view of the public's expectations, the NRA had proved itself a tragic failure. Since the previous May, the trend of production and employment, of bank clearings and other major business indices, had been downward. Relief was being pared while there still remained some eleven million unemployed. Millions of workers were without collective bargaining through representatives of their own choosing, and even before the national textile shutdown, thousands had been blacklisted for resorting to strikes. Johnson's insistence on the right to limit production and fix prices had brought the whole recovery effort to a desperate crisis. Most labor leaders now viewed him as a violent man, the one who had whipped up the vigilantes of San Francisco. Nor could they ignore his perversion of Section 7a and its guarantee of collective-bargaining rights in the precedent-setting automobile code.

Even in industry many had become disenchanted with Johnson's mercurial leadership. The United States Chamber of Commerce was opposed to the extension or reenactment of the NRA, insisting that government should no longer take any part in the development of industry codes, but merely approve or veto those developed by industrial management. And try as they might, neither the General nor Richberg could undo the overall damage inflicted on the NRA by the highly publicized indictments of the Darrow Review Board.

Within days of Johnson's belligerent Carnegie Hall attack upon the striking textile workers in mid-September, and his unwarranted use of the name of Supreme Court Justice Louis D. Brandeis to bulwark an untenable position on the reorganization of NRA, the President finally acted. After directing Richberg to draw up a draft letter praising the General for his hard work and loyalty, and granting him a leave of absence through mid-October, the Chief Executive accepted Johnson's resignation as administrator of the NRA.

Undated duplicate of a draft by Richberg, with handwritten insertion "F 6/20/34," and typed in the upper-left-hand corner the notation "the original of this document has been retired for preservation"; Johnson to FDR, June 26, 1934; telegraphic memorandums from Stephen Early to McIntyre, August 27, 30, 31, 1934; Richberg to FDR, September 4, 1934; Richberg to McIntyre, September 5, 1934; Tugwell to FDR, August [sic] 5, 1934, with "August" lined out and "Sept." inserted in FDR's handwriting; Tugwell to FDR, September 7, 1934; Richberg to FDR, September 14, 1934; all of the preceding from Roosevelt Papers, OF 466; *New York Times,* August 19, 21, 29, September 26, 1934; Schlesinger, *The Coming of the New Deal,* 152–56; Hawley, *The New Deal and the Problem of Monopoly,* 104–5; Johnson, *The Blue Eagle,* 212, 214, 371–97; Perkins, *The Roosevelt I Knew,* 235–49; Richberg, *My Hero,* 174–76, 178–81; Vadney, *The Wayward Liberal,* 136–44.

7

Farewell to the NRA

WITH JOHNSON removed, the President sought to reorganize and revitalize the NRA's administrative structure. On September 27, he created a new National Industrial Recovery Board (NIRB), and soon designated S. Clay Williams, a Southern conservative and onetime president of the R. J. Reynolds Tobacco Company, as chairman. The other board members were Arthur D. Whiteside, a former NRA division administrator, previously president of Dun and Bradstreet, to represent business; Sidney Hillman of the Amalgamated Clothing Workers to speak for labor; and two college professors, Leon C. Marshall and Walton H. Hamilton, to represent the public and the consumer. The NIRB was to assume Johnson's key administrative duties. An Industrial Emergency Committee, directed by Richberg, was assigned the task of formulating policy for all recovery agencies.

At the end of October, in an endeavor to halt the continuing deterioration within NRA, the President announced another major reorganization. This time, he created a new National Emergency Council, headed by Richberg, and combined in this single agency all the advisory bodies which had been activated the previous month, along with the original National Emergency Council. Included on the new Council were Cabinet officers and the executive heads of major permanent and relief agencies. With great fanfare from the White House, Richberg was assigned such sweeping powers that one perceptive observer concluded they were too great for any one man, or any single piece of government machinery, no matter how large or smooth-running. To the great irritation of Roosevelt and some Cabinet members, Richberg was soon hailed by headline-oriented newsmen as the new Assistant President.

Once viewed with hostility by industrial magnates, Richberg had become one of their favorites. Before audiences throughout the country, he insisted that the New Deal had halted the forces of communism and anarchism. He spoke out against enactment of a thirty-hour-work-week bill, and persistently stressed the primary importance of restoring business confidence and encouraging management through the limitation of regulatory legislation.

Shortly after the National Labor Relations Board rejected the President's interpretation of Section 7a in the automobile settlement of March 25, 1934, and ruled, in the Houde Engineering Corporation case in the late summer of 1934, that Section 7a provided that the representatives of the majority should constitute the exclusive agency for collective bargaining with the employer, Richberg reaffirmed his support for the proportional representation of employees in collective bargaining. When the NLRB, in a related case, charged a San Francisco newspaper with violating Section 7a, Richberg came down hard on the side of the publisher and convinced the President to weaken the jurisdiction of the NLRB in the newspaper industry.[1] At a meeting of the Iron and Steel Institute, Richberg gave his blessing to the renewal of the steel code, with all its highly criticized unsound price controls and basing-point clauses. And finally, as guest speaker at the annual dinner of the National Association of Manufacturers, he reaffirmed his support for industrial self-government, and urged that the fundamental principles of the NRA, including the much-disputed codes of fair competition, be preserved in permanent legislation.

The new format of the NRA proved too cumbersome; it was awkward and unworkable. Over the weeks and months which followed, there was no perceptible change in general policy. De-

1. Rodney Carlisle, "William Randolph Hearst's Reaction to the American Newspaper Guild: A Challenge to New Deal Labor Legislation," *Labor History*, X (Winter 1969), 74–90, 98–99.

spite increasing pressure for major modification of the codes from the Research and Planning Division, the Consumers' Advisory Board, and the Federal Trade Commission, Richberg and his conservative allies, Williams and Whiteside, fought off the advocates of change, and rejected liberal Brain Trusters as key NRA appointees. In only two major instances during the next eight months did the NIRB act against the wishes of business. The overall results were a continued stalemate between competing internal forces, and a marked tendency by the NIRB to maintain the status quo and to respond sympathetically to business complaints. There was, therefore, no fundamental difference from the Johnson era. Believing that new administrative leadership would solve the basic problems confronting the NRA, Richberg and Williams rejected major policy alterations, but did resort to a gentler and more diplomatic approach to labor and industry.

Exec. Order No. 6889-A, October 29, 1934; Richberg, *The Rainbow,* 74–75, 183, 191–93; Schlesinger, *The Coming of the New Deal,* 157–58, 398–400; Harold L. Ickes, *Secret Diary,* (3 vols., New York, 1953–54), I, *The First Thousand Days, 1933–1936,* 198, 200–1, 209–11, 219–20, 235–36, 242–43, 245–47; *New Republic,* October 10, 1934, 230, April 24, 1935, 301–4; *New York Times,* July 6, September 28, October 1, 3, 5, 6, 9, 10, 12, 14, 22, November 23, December 14, 18, 23, 1934; Richberg to FDR, September 4, 14, 1934, and Tugwell to FDR, September 5, 7, 1934, Roosevelt Papers, OF 466; *Code Authorities and Their Part in the Administration of NIRA,* 190; United States Senate, Committee on Finance, *Investigation of the National Recovery Administration* (74th Cong., 1st sess., 1935), 940–61; Hawley, *The New Deal and the Problem of Monopoly,* 106–10; Vadney, *The Wayward Liberal,* 146–50.

Richberg Fails the NRA

Richberg's success as "chief of staff" depended entirely on the support given him by Roosevelt. When it became evident that he did not enjoy the full confidence of the President, that more aggressive officials gained easier access to the Chief Executive, and that he was merely carrying out presidential orders, Richberg quickly lost influence with others. Not long after his appointment to head the NEC, policies were made and approved by the President without Richberg's knowledge. "Department heads found they could ignore him with impunity."

His prestige and his usefulness soon plummeted, for he was unable to coordinate the many New Deal agencies, to reduce the confusion surrounding the NRA, or to endear himself to government or labor spokesmen. Furthermore, he permitted himself to look ridiculous when, in December 1934, he voiced undue alarm to Johnson and the *Saturday Evening Post* over the magazine's forthcoming publication of the General's memoirs. In March 1935, the usually eloquent Richberg adopted an untenable position when, during an appearance before the Senate Finance Committee, he suddenly charged Senator Borah with favoring monopolies. This accusation was incomprehensible; the Idaho senator had consistently assailed the NRA for suspending the antitrust laws and benefiting big industry at the expense of the smaller businessman. Having alienated the spokesmen of labor, Richberg now made firm enemies of the progressive bloc in Congress. And he had not done well by the President or the nation.

Early in 1935, the NRA's Research and Planning Division concluded that real wages had not increased to any significant extent, if at all, since the advent of the codes. Workingmen's wages had risen about 6 percent between June 1933 and November 1934. But advances in retail prices during that same period had more than offset the small gain in dollar wages. Accordingly, the Research and Planning statisticians concluded that real wages in January 1935 were about the same as they had been twelve months earlier, and below those of June 1933.

Although additional public hearings were held early in 1935 on prices, there was no major change in NRA policy or in the lines of battle within the organization. The continued stalemate insured that NRA officials would hesitate to enforce code provisions which ran counter to such controversial policy pronouncements as Office Memorandum 228. This hesitation, in turn, facilitated a breakdown and then voluntary abandonment of controls and price schedules in lumber, retail and service trades, tires, plumbing fixtures, and the mackerel industry.

Seligman and Cornwell, eds., *New Deal Mosaic,* 232–474; Herman M. Somers, *Presidential Agency: The Office of War Mobilization and Reconversion* (Cambridge, Mass., 1950), 206–08; Mangold in *New Republic,* May 22, 1935, 48; *New York Times,* November 2, December 18, 1934; January 10, 11, 1935; *Blue Eagle* [NRA house organ], January 16, 1935; Senate Finance Committee, *Investigation of the National Recovery Administration,* 892–93; Hawley, *The New Deal and the Problem of Monopoly,* 111–15.

A Progressive Mandate: For a New NIRA?

In the months leading up to the Congressional elections of November 1934, Democratic candidates were assisted by outdated appeals from Old Guard Republicans, and by hysterical charges hurled by the newly born American Liberty League, an organization of conservatives and businessmen. Instead of the normal midterm swing away from the party in power, the election resulted in disaster for the Republican candidates. Despite the continued depression, vast numbers of voters were apparently determined not to return to the bankruptcy, empty phrases, and negativism of the Republicans, or to the bankers and businessmen who had failed them since 1929. This overwhelming endorsement of the vigor and experimentation of the New Deal seemed to indicate that the public was prepared to go even further than Roosevelt.

The only electoral gains by non-Democratic candidates were those of progressive forces to the left of the President. Wisconsin voters gave young Bob La Follette a smashing victory in his progressive campaign for reelection to the Senate, while Farmer-Laborite Governor Floyd Olson strengthened his hold on Minnesota. In Connecticut, the Socialist candidate for governor swept the industrial city of Bridgeport, and a number of party members were elected to the state legislature. Almost everywhere, conservative Republicans were rejected decisively by their constituencies.

The President felt strengthened by this mandate, which one newspaper described as the most overwhelming victory in the history of American politics. The Democrats in the Seventy-fourth Congress now had a majority of 45 seats in the Senate and 219 in the House, with the progressive initiative being transferred to the Senate. Congress henceforth afforded the Chief Executive and his policies greater support, except for the NRA.

By the end of 1934, Richberg had still made no progress in revitalizing the NRA. Confusion and disintegration had reached such a stage that increasing numbers of its friends concluded that the NIRA had best be allowed to expire the following June with its good features being preserved through separate enactments. The President did seem committed to establishing a permanent NRA, but with concessions to those who opposed price-fixing, price cutting, or the control of production. Conceding that the "evangelistic" phase was at an end, he now looked forward to the easing of the more stringent business regulations.

Some of the President's close friends in the Senate, including members of the progressive group, felt that any attempt to revive the NRA along the old lines was futile. Furthermore, it should have been clear that no plan for long-range reorganization was feasible until the Supreme Court ruled on at least one of the cases in which lower courts had challenged its constitutionality.

Storm warnings of continued disintegration within the NRA were revived in late March 1935 with the resignation of S. Clay Williams. Ineffective as an administrator, the retiring chairman of the National Industrial Recovery Board had by this time become thoroughly unpopular with progressives and with labor leaders. Richberg continued to urge upon Roosevelt administrative reorganization, not policy changes. The failures of the

NIRB under Williams and Richberg had further discredited the NRA, and the result was an observable increase in consumer alienation and a decided rise in industrial and business violations of the wage and hour provisions of codes.

New York Times, November 7, 1934; Richberg to FDR, March 25, May 1, 1935, Roosevelt Papers, OF 466; Schlesinger, *The Coming of the New Deal,* 163–65.

The Senate Responds

The legislative outlook was bleak, particularly in the Senate. By mid-March, it seemed highly unlikely that any constructive bill for the renewal of the NRA would emanate from Congress. A discouraged Richberg concluded that the only thing that could save the NRA was appointment of a new, knowledgeable chairman with the full backing of the White House. Of course, Richberg deemed himself the knowledgeable candidate. Although he had been generally regarded as the actual head of the NRA since the removal of Johnson, Richberg now conceded that he lacked adequate authority to do the job. With Williams' resignation, he asked the President either to assign him to the vacant position, so that he would be empowered to fulfill his public obligations, or to give the necessary authority to someone else in whom he had confidence.

On March 21, 1935, Roosevelt designated Richberg the new chairman of the National Industrial Recovery Board and appointed an industry representative to fill the spot vacated by Williams. When Whiteside resigned, he was replaced by Charles Edison of Edison Industries. But the distressing situation was not altered. There was a spreading defiance of the codes, and FDR was obliged to make decisions on problems which should never have reached him from NRA subordinates, including Richberg. Furthermore, Richberg made it clear that he would not alter any policy until Congress had determined the future of the NIRA, which was due to expire on June 16.

In spite of these disheartening developments, the President

decided to seek Congressional extension of a modified NRA for two years and to press for a speedy court decision on a new case. Altering an earlier neutralist position the Chief Executive, in a typical Rooseveltian compromise, had sent a special message to Congress on February 20. He recommended retention of Section 7a without important change, restriction of future price and production controls to protect small business, and the use of the antitrust laws against monopolies and price-fixing. This message had been drafted largely by Richberg, after consultation with Senators Harrison and Wagner. It had the support of Green and Lewis because Section 7a was to be retained. Senate opposition to extension of the NRA coalesced around old-line progressives like Borah and Nye, and economic conservatives like Carter Glass of Virginia, a Wilsonian Democrat. Back in 1933, Glass had successfully defied Johnson by refusing to put the Blue Eagle on his newspapers.

The Administration was on the defensive from the start. The Borah-Nye-Glass coalition pushed through an investigation of the NRA by the Senate Finance Committee, and what resulted was more than 2,400 pages of conflicting testimony, presented in what amounted to a series of Field Days of Criticism: Retail, consumer, and farm spokesmen, and authorities such as Darrow, indicted the monopolistic tendencies of the NRA, while Johnson and others insisted that it had helped the "little fellow" by outlawing price-cutting.

The Senate coalition opposing the Blue Eagle was given some timely help by the esteemed Brookings Institution when it released a devastating study of the NRA.

In almost a thousand pages of detailed substantiation and careful analysis, these Brookings economists, some of them former NRA staff members, reported on the impact of the NRA codes upon the nation. After according due recognition to the purpose of the President, to the "psychological lift" that the NRA had afforded at the beginning, and to its elimination of certain undesirable employment conditions and business practices, the Brookings group recognized the inevitable shortcomings of a hastily improvised and ambitious undertaking. The damning conclusions were crystal clear—the defects of the code machinery were so serious "as to be irremediable without abolishing the codes themselves," for the NRA had retarded recovery, injured the wage earner, and diminished the volume of production.

Confirming most of the criticisms which had been leveled at the NRA by its own Consumers' Advisory Board and Research and Planning Division, by the Federal Trade Commission, and by individual critics such as Paul H. Douglas and Norman Thomas, the Brookings Report concluded that there had been no increase in the purchasing power of the average employed worker, for living costs had risen as fast as income. Only one-sixth of the unemployed had been given jobs, these mainly the result of a share-work program involving the shortening of hours. Since profits had risen faster than wage earnings, there had been no favorable alteration of the pre-New Deal distribution of total income between wages and property incomes. Employment had been limited by the failure of production to increase—the result of higher prices charged by industry and of limitations of output by the codes. Prices that were already too high, for such products as steel and building materials, had been further increased under the codes.

The report also underscored the inconsistent and dysfunctional roles played by Roosevelt, Johnson, and Richberg in their interpretation of the collective-bargaining sections of the NIRA. The failure of the Administration to enforce decisions by the NLB and its successor, the NLRB, in important cases had contributed to the extensive labor dissatisfaction and strikes of the time. Some of the codes had proven so unworkable with respect to minimum wages and maximum hours that they were unenforceable and made chiseling inevitable. Labor had gained only in the few cases where it was well organized and effectively led, and consumers, lacking organization, had secured practically nothing.

The report indicted Roosevelt and his administration for

having no overall plan and no integrated policy. The result had been that "working at high speed under a statute that gave little guidance, and without clear standards of its own, it enacted into law a huge mass of rules and regulations arrived at by a process of bargaining among conflicting interests." Meanwhile, the government of industry had been turned over, without plan and without check, to an assortment of private profit-seeking groups. And the result, overall, was a strengthening of pre-existing trends toward monopoly, profiteering, and an economy of scarcity.[2]

The effect of this crushing report was to shatter what remained of a potentially large bloc of Senate votes committed to extension of a revised NRA. The Senate Finance Committee then proceeded to cut the heart out of the President's proposal. It substituted a resolution, by Senator Clark of Missouri, limiting NRA operations to interstate business, forbidding price-fixing except in mineral-resource industries, and extending its life for only ten months, to April 1, 1936. On May 14, 1935, the Senate approved the Clark resolution by voice vote.

Thus, barely two weeks before the Supreme Court would hand down its ruling in the Schechter case, voiding Title I of the NIRA, the Senate entombed what little remained of the NRA. Trade and industry would have no fear in resisting whatever was left of government pressure, knowing that the revised NRA lacked adequate legal authority to impose any code. And competent personnel would not be available for a mere ten-month endeavor. What remained was so ineffective and unworkable that Richberg felt the President would suffer less and the country benefit more if the NRA was killed outright. Richberg let it be known that he would return to private life by June 16, the day the original NIRA was to expire.

In the House of Representatives, meanwhile, Congressman Robert L. Doughton introduced a new Administration measure on May 16. It proposed a two-year extension of the NIRA,

2. Lyon et al., *The National Recovery Administration*, 79–82, 137–40, 256–58, 287–88, 289–99, 395–409, 527–48, 743–48, 871–75.

applicable to all industries engaged in interstate commerce, permitted price-fixing when necessary to stop discriminatory price cutting and sought to protect small enterprises, halt the growth of monopolies, and conserve natural resources. On May 20, the Ways and Means Committee initiated hearings on the proposal, which seemed likely to pass on the date scheduled for a House vote, May 28. The previous day, however, a unanimous Supreme Court intervened.

Schlesinger, *The Coming of the New Deal,* 167–72, 544–49; Richberg, *My Hero,* 185–88; Richberg to FDR, March 25, April 12, 13, 26, May 1, 1935, and FDR to Richberg, March 25, 1935, Roosevelt Papers, OF 466; *New York Times,* January 23, 24, February 1, 3, 4, 7, 16, 21, March 1, 6–11, 15, 16, 21, 22, 27, April 26, May 2, 3, 11, 15–19, 20–26, 28, 1935; Senate Finance Committee, *Investigation of the NRA,* 300–10, 524–36, 591–98, 661–68, 809–15, 849–57, 999–1004, 1183–96, 1247–70, 1711–24, 2437–50.

The Courts Respond to a Sick Chicken

Roosevelt had been confronted with a conscious Johnson-Richberg policy of delaying a court test, at least until the NRA had proved itself. The Administration, however, finally bowed to increasing Congressional opposition by permitting the Belcher case, involving violations of the lumber and timber products code, to work its way up to the Supreme Court early in 1935. Though Felix Frankfurter urged Roosevelt to delay resort to the courts, and seemed to have won when the Department of Justice withdrew the Belcher litigation in late March, Richberg himself now set the judicial wheels in motion once more. Responding to newspaper charges that the NRA did not dare face a judicial test, the new NIRB chairman got the Department of Justice, in the absence of a vacationing Roosevelt, to submit a new test case to the Supreme Court in early April. Before the end of the month, Attorney General Homer S. Cummings, who was not in complete sympathy with the NRA, appointed Richberg to collaborate with Solicitor General Stanley F. Reed to argue the case of the A. L. A. Schechter Poultry Corporation before the Supreme Court.

The four Schechter brothers were the largest suppliers in Brooklyn, New York, of kosher poultry to Jewish customers. In October 1934, the federal district court found them guilty on nineteen counts, including disregarding wage and hour regulations, filing false reports, and selling unfit and uninspected poultry. In April 1935, the circuit court, on appeal, sustained conviction on seventeen of the counts.

On May 2–3, counsel for the Schechters argued before the United States Supreme Court that the code system amounted to the unconstitutional delegation of legislative powers, that their business was outside the scope of Congress in its regulation of interstate commerce, and that they were being deprived of liberty and property without due process of law. Relying heavily on a broad definition of the power of Congress to regulate interstate commerce, Richberg maintained that the critical emergency created by the Great Depression gave the President and the Congress the right to act on a national scale with a new interpretation of the scope of federal regulation. The traditional, negative approach of the antitrust laws had to be replaced by positive policies like those laid down by the NRA codes, which filled the gap when Congress found itself unable to establish guidelines for individual industries.

On May 27, Chief Justice Charles Evans Hughes sent shock waves through the nation when he made it crystal clear that the Supreme Court rejected Richberg's reasoning. Insisting that "Extraordinary conditions do not create or enlarge constitutional power," the nine justices in *United States* v. *A. L. A. Schechter Poultry Corporation,* unanimously voided Title I of the NIRA, including Section 7a, as an invalid delegation of legislative power to the President, and an unconstitutional regulation of intrastate transactions with only an indirect effect upon interstate commerce. The Court held that the transactions of the Schechter brothers—purchasing in New York City chickens which had been raised in other states, and transporting them to Brooklyn for slaughter and final local sale—were outside the "current" or "flow" of interstate commerce, and therefore not subject to the regulatory power of Congress. The Court observed that Congress could regulate matters which, though purely intrastate themselves, affected interstate commerce, but that power might be invoked only when the effect was direct. The NRA attempt to fix hours and wages in the intrastate business of the Schechter brothers was an invalid exercise of the commerce power.

With the nullification of the Recovery Act, the slate was wiped clean and the antitrust laws were once more in effect.

New York Times, March 3, 27, April 2, 5, May 28, 1935; Schlesinger, *The Age of Roosevelt,* III, *The Politics of Upheaval,* 274–83; Richberg, *The Rainbow,* 209–14, 217–41; Richberg to FDR, April 3, 1935, and Reed to FDR, April 11, 1935, Roosevelt Papers, OF 466; Hawley, *The New Deal and the Problem of Monopoly,* 127–28; Vadney, *The Wayward Liberal,* 161–67.

A New Labor Policy

In view of the overwhelming New Deal victory in the 1934 Congressional elections, and the utter inadequacy of existing legislation to protect the right of workers to bargain collectively, it seemed incredible to labor and progressive spokesmen that the President persisted in his refusal to endorse Wagner's Labor Disputes Bill, first introduced in March 1934. Had he at once pushed hard for enactment of the original bill, and been successful, most of the distressing vacillation of the Administration on labor questions might have been averted. The debilitating controversy over the automobile settlement could have been prevented, vital decisions by the NLRB could not have been reversed by the President, and, finally, the meaning of Section 7a would have been clarified for all.

Introduced in the Senate on February 21, 1935 as S. 1958, Wagner's revised bill replaced the generalized statements of Section 7a with a comprehensive labor statute outlawing specific unfair labor practices, such as company unions and other employer tactics which interfered with collective bargaining; provided for a permanent National Labor Relations Board with power comparable to that of the Federal Trade Commission to proceed on its own initiative against violators; and gave legal sanction to the right of an employee majority to choose collective-bargaining representatives for the whole group, as defined in the Houde decision.

The great debate on the Wagner proposal occurred in the Senate Committee on Education and Labor between March 11 and April 2, with little left to be said on the Senate floor or in the House of Representatives. It had already been discussed for more than a year in Congress, in the press, and on the radio. The testifying witnesses duplicated those involved in the 1934 debate, with the business community solidly opposed to the bill, along with the Communist party, while the NLRB, the trade unions, the Socialist party, and religious leaders aligned in support of it.

The National Association of Manufacturers resorted to every means of communication and lobbying imaginable in an endeavor to kill the bill. The Chamber of Commerce, meeting in Washington on May 2, 1935, finally broke with Roosevelt, not only rejecting the Wagner proposal but denouncing the New Deal in its entirety. With organized business in complete opposition, the path was laid open for the President to make a decisive move in labor's direction.

On the same day that the Chamber of Commerce broke with FDR, the Senate Committee on Education and Labor unanimously reported out Wagner's bill, including Francis Biddle's suggestion making it an unfair practice for an employer to refuse to bargain collectively with representatives of his employees. Senator Wagner finally convinced FDR not to intervene and to permit the Senate to vote freely on the bill. Wagner was now confident of the outcome.

With Roosevelt no longer blocking the way, and catalyzed by the 1934 Congressional elections, progressive forces joined the well-organized lobbying endeavors of a labor movement at the height of its influence and got S. 1958 passed by a crushing 63 to 12 vote. Those senators who had little enthusiasm for the bill, but feared facing a hostile AF of L at the polls, voted in the affirmative in the expectation that the Supreme Court would declare it unconstitutional.

Confronted with the possibility of losing his legislative leadership in the House—and encountering conflicting attitudes toward the bill among the members of his own administration, including outright opposition from Richberg—FDR finally decided to endorse Wagner's bill on May 24. Three days later, the nine members of the Supreme Court unanimously handed down the Schechter decision.

New York Times, September 13, October 12, 16, November 17, 21, 1934; May 25, 1935; Bernstein, *New Deal Collective Bargaining Policy,* 87, 90–99; Lorwin and Wubnig, *Labor Relations Boards,* Ch. XI; Green to FDR, February 11, 1935, Roosevelt Papers, OF 466; Huthmacher, *Senator Robert F. Wagner,* 195–98; Bernstein, *Turbulent Years,* 330–42, 344–49.

The NRA Is Retired

Ironically, the battered Blue Eagle found more friends in death than it had during its lifetime, as one journalist put it. Progressive critics who had attacked the NRA for failing to raise real wages hoped that Congress would speedily enact new legislation to preserve the concepts of minimum wages, maximum hours, and the abolition of child labor, as developed under NRA codes. Appalled by the Court's decision, the AF of L disclosed, within days, reports streaming in from all parts of the country of wage cuts and increases in the work week. Although a number of large firms responded positively to appeals for voluntary retention of code agreements, it was inevitable that the usual ruthless minorities would reduce prices by cutting labor costs, and thus affect entire industries. NRA headquarters soon reported large-scale chiseling throughout the country, with smaller firms the chief culprits. The possible return of cutthroat tactics disconcerted many of the very businessmen who, in prior months, had complained bitterly that the NRA was depriving them of their liberties. Those individuals devoted to the abolition of child labor viewed the Court decision as a body blow, and worried about the poor prospects of their proposed constitutional amendment as a replacement. Even Wall Street experienced an adverse reaction, for stock-market prices turned downward within twenty-four hours and continued to sag for the remainder of that week.

On the same Monday that the NIRA was voided, the Court overturned the Frazier-Lemke farm-mortgage-moratorium law, and ruled that the President had exceeded his powers in forcing the resignation of William E. Humphries from the Federal Trade Commission. It was an eventful, emotional day for Roosevelt, and he showed his feelings later that week when he denounced the Court for taking the nation back to "the horse and buggy days of 1789" and for depriving its central government of control over the social and economic conditions affecting the welfare of the entire population.

But had the court nullified a viable law? And had it denied Roosevelt the opportunity to confront the social and economic problems of the nation with more advanced planning and more enlightened legislation?

By the time the Supreme Court declared the NIRA unconstitutional, virtually all progressives in New Deal circles opposed it, while their less liberal colleagues had come to view it as more of a headache than an effective weapon with which to revive the nation. Monopolistic developments under the NRA, as well as enforcement difficulties, had made a farce of the "voluntary" character of the venture. Overall, the NRA had been a dismal failure. The Supreme Court had merely hammered the last nail into the coffin.

On June 4, the President convened an emergency meeting of Congressional leaders at the White House. At that time, Roosevelt reluctantly conceded the death of the NRA, and permitted it to be laid to rest by passage of Senator Clark's resolution and affirming legislation. But he was also determined that the New Deal program encompassed in Section 7a and the code labor standards would be preserved in substitute enactments.

FDR was pushed toward support of the Wagner bill and other progressive legislation in 1935 by the results of the Congressional elections in November 1934 and by the determination and foresight of Robert F. Wagner. In addition, he was influenced by the violent antagonism of the Chamber of Commerce, the NAM, and the American Liberty League, the failure of the NRA experiment in self-government in industry, and the fortuitous timing of the Schechter decision.

Although Wagner was convinced that the Court's ruling did not fundamentally challenge the constitutionality of his bill, he nevertheless made certain revisions in its policy statement and definitions, and reordered some paragraphs, especially to avoid basing the authority assigned to Congress by the bill exclusively on its power to regulate interstate commerce. With the President's vigorous support at every step of the way thereafter, the House passed the bill without a roll call on June 19, and the House and Senate accepted the conference report on June 27, the former by a vote of 132 to 42, and the latter without a roll call. On July 5, the President affixed his signature to what became known as the National Labor Relations Act, afterward giving the pens to Wagner and Green.

A month earlier, the President had been handed the resignation of a "mentally fagged and physically depressed" Richberg, who felt that very little more could be accomplished to save the great values of the NRA. Feeling more of a burden than an aid to Roosevelt, the chairman of the National Industrial Recovery Board retired. And so did the NRA.[3]

3. A joint resolution, approved on June 14, 1935, theoretically extended until April 1, 1936, Title I of the Recovery Act, but in an emasculated form, for it repealed those parts of the original act that delegated power to the President to approve or prescribe codes of fair competition and that provided for the enforcement of such codes. A few of the divisions continued operations, but on a greatly diminished scale. The NRA was formally terminated on January 1, 1936, when some units

New York Times, May 28, 29, June 5, 1935; Richberg to FDR, June 5, 1935, Roosevelt Papers, OF 466; Bernstein, *New Deal Collective Bargaining Policy,* 121–27.

were transferred to the Department of Commerce for liquidation by the following April 1, and the Consumers' Division was shunted to the Department of Labor.

8

Some Final Thoughts

IN A BELATED ENDEAVOR to overcome the most serious domestic crisis since the Civil War, Franklin D. Roosevelt in 1933 urged Congress to adopt a hastily developed omnibus measure, in the hope that it would revive the nation's economy and preserve its human and natural resources. Members of Congress ignored the lessons of history as well as the warnings of old-line populist-progressive colleagues, and through Title I of the National Industrial Recovery Act, delegated unlimited decision-making power to an unborn bureaucracy, with minimal clarity as to standards, guidelines, or principles. Policy making was left essentially an administrative prerogative, with the result that further power was delegated to the industrial and commercial sectors of society.

In essence, Title I of the NIRA turned much of the nation's power over to highly organized, well-financed trade associations and industrial combines. This was achieved through the regulation of prices and wages, the extension of monopolistic practices, and the elimination of the closed shop and of the rule of the majority in collective bargaining. The unorganized public, otherwise known as the consumer, along with the members of the fledgling trade-union movement, had virtually nothing to say about the initial organization of the National Recovery Administration, or the formulation of basic policy.

Neither Congress nor the President seriously faced up to the task of directing, let alone controlling, the administrative agency created by an irascible Hugh Johnson in Washington, and the individual code authorities that sprouted on all sides. Theoretically, organization and control of this new bureaucracy had been left in the hands of those most directly affected. The actual developments insured violations of, or serious inroads into, our system of countervailing forces, of checks and balances. As James Madison once put it, "You must first enable the government to control the governed, and in the next place oblige it to control itself."

John Kenneth Galbraith has at times contended that countervailing powers usually crop up somewhere, somehow, but in this instance the organized business interests kept major control of the NRA. The White House permitted the National Association of Manufacturers, the Chamber of Commerce, and allied business and trade associations to assume overriding authority. And the fact that these associations were often homogeneous in their aspirations, expectations, and tactical approach to issues and programs facilitated their speedy dominance. In contrast, trade unions and the consumer remained disorganized and generally ineffective in their endeavors to balance the power of business and industry. Indeed, private administration became public administration, and private government became public government, insuring the marriage of capitalism with statism.

The long, heartbreaking struggle of this country's working men and women to regain a position of dignity as human beings, and to end, once and for all, the destructive plagues of industrial feudalism, was not completed with the early years of the New Deal. As a pragmatist and an adherent of consensus politics, Franklin D. Roosevelt was prepared to ease, but not abolish on his own initiative, the disheartening inequities which had afflicted generations of American workers.

Where organized labor was weak, Roosevelt was unprepared to withstand the pressures of industrial spokesmen to control the writing, as well as the administering, of NRA codes. Nor was the President able, or willing, to offset the effective efforts of highly organized industries to crush the strikes of weakened unions with the collusion of conservative public officials and the resort to military and police forces. Only those unions whose leadership displayed imagination, commitment, courage, and independence, were in a position to overcome the opposition of industry-oriented administrators like Richberg, Johnson and the latter's underlings on the NRA staff. The hesitant unions which relied on a paternalistic government, and the fearful, conservative leadership in the American Federation of Labor, failed to take lasting advantage of some of the opportunities afforded by Section 7a of the NIRA.

Under the NRA, strikes continued to be broken, pickets continued to be imprisoned or slain, and the dreams and aspirations of union members continued to be shattered. The bitterness and hatred toward an independent labor movement which had persistently engulfed powerful industry spokesmen was not significantly eased during these early years under Roosevelt. The door to labor's rights was slightly opened, but the unyielding determination of progressive lawmakers like New York's Robert F. Wagner, Wisconsin's Robert M. LaFollette, Jr., and Nebraska's George W. Norris, would be needed to push FDR and Congress toward a more enlightened approach in the unending struggle to regain for the working class a position of dignity in a more humane and democratic society.

The NRA tended, during its brief existence, to renew the hopes of many workers, and facilitated a much-needed reappraisal of the distressing relationships between labor and management which had scarred this nation since the advent of the industrial revolution.

Had FDR been a closer observer of history, he might have recalled that his distant cousin Theodore Roosevelt sought to create, during his presidency, a government in Washington that would be independent of, and superior to, big business. Viewing himself as a pragmatist, however, FDR surrendered an inordinate share of the power of government, through the NRA, to industrial spokesmen throughout the country. He never seemed to realize that the NRA was a poor use, if not abuse, of this power. Not until these same business leaders, and their Liberty League allies, revived by the NRA, denounced him in a general chorus, and subsequent to the Supreme Court's voiding of Title I of the NIRA, did FDR seek a new, more progressive and pro-labor consensus.

After the Supreme Court's nullification of the NRA, and its abandonment by Congress, Roosevelt created a new coalition of interests and assumed increased leadership and power. Labor, for example, was given the National Labor Relations Act of 1935, which, at most, provided a "more friendly milieu within which to bargain and fight." And the passage of the Fair Labor Standards Act of 1938 strengthened labor in its struggle for existence and for human dignity.

Bibliographic Essay

<hr>

~~~~~~

Private Papers and Government Collections

Several of the key manuscript collections for this period are at the Franklin D. Roosevelt Library at Hyde Park, New York. These include the Franklin D. Roosevelt Papers, for the exchange of correspondence, reports, and memorandums between FDR, Johnson, Richberg, Perkins, and other Cabinet and key staff members in the White House; the Leon Henderson manuscripts; and the Rexford G. Tugwell manuscripts. Other useful manuscript collections are those of Donald R. Richberg, at the Library of Congress; Norman Thomas, at the New York Public Library; Robert F. Wagner, at Georgetown University; and Gerard Swope, at Columbia University.

The Columbia University Oral History Collection contains tape-recorded interviews with significant reference to the NRA and its leadership, including those of Rexford G. Tugwell, Henry A. Wallace (available November 1975), James P. Warburg, Frances Perkins (available May 1975), Thomas I. Emerson, Jerome N. Frank, William H. Davis, and M. L. Wilson.

Public documents and government publications are vital to an understanding of the background of this period, and the developments relating to the NRA. There is great significance to the hearings of the House of Representatives on the thirty-hour bill, Congressional hearings on the National Industrial Recovery proposal, and the heated floor debates as reported in the *Congressional Record*. There are hundreds of clarifying economic documents developed by staff members of the NRA, dealing with such significant issues as price regulation, employment and unemployment, price filing, overlapping of codes, and the role of code authorities in the administration of the NIRA. Also helpful to an understanding of business and consumer reactions and grievances are the NRA hearings on administration of the codes of fair practices, and the *Proceedings of the National Emergency Council*. The reports submitted by the majority and minority members of the National Recovery Review

Board, headed by Clarence Darrow, display a disturbing haste and extreme partisanship, as do the rebuttals of Donald Richberg and his staff, but they are instructive. Finally, there is the United States Senate, Committee on Finance, *Investigation of the National Recovery Administration* (74th Cong., 1st sess., 1935).

The records of the National Recovery Administration in the National Archives belong to Record Group 9 and amount to some six thousand cubic feet of material. Most of these records were transferred from the Department of Commerce as early as 1940. These do not include personnel records, which are now stored in the Federal Records Center in St. Louis.

A comprehensive administrative history of the NRA, including a description of its records, is found in *Preliminary Inventories, Records of the National Recovery Administration,* No. 44, National Archives (226 pp., Washington, D. C., 1952). These records contain information on basic economic problems involving raw-material supplies, labor, production, distribution, trade practices, and prices, on individual industries, on local problems and conditions, and on specific firms. A former NRA official once concluded that prior to the Second World War, these records constituted "the largest and richest single body of information concerning the problems and operation of industry ever assembled in any nation." NRA personnel, for example, produced more than 2,500 economic studies, some for limited distribution, others in typescript only.

In 1954, the National Archives issued *Special Lists, Select List of Documents in the Records of the National Recovery Administration,* No. 12 (190 pp., Washington, D. C.), which cites reports and studies organized into series by the NRA and the Department of Commerce, along with additional materials selected for their significance by the staff of the National Archives. The Document Series of basic materials relating to individual codes is not included in this list but is available as Microfilm Publication No. 213 of the National Archives.

Personal Accounts

Among the useful memoirs, autobiographies, and analyses written by those involved in the development of the NIRA, and its execution by the NRA, are Francis B. Biddle, *In Brief Authority* (Garden City, N. Y., 1962); Harold L. Ickes, *Secret Diary,* (3 vols., New York, 1953–4), I, *The First Thousand Days, 1933–1936;* and

Hugh S. Johnson, *The Blue Eagle from Egg to Earth* (Garden City, N. Y., 1935). In Leverett S. Lyon et al., *The National Recovery Administration, Analysis and Appraisal* (Washington, D. C., 1935), the authors analyze the NRA and show that it tended to work against recovery. Raymond Moley worked with FDR in forming the Brain Trust, but there was divergency in their public opinions during the first seven years of FDR's presidency, and this is shown in his *After Seven Years* (New York, 1939). Moley's *The First New Deal* (New York, 1966) is the best of the conservative critiques. Also useful are *Frances Perkins, *The Roosevelt I Knew* (New York, 1946) and two books by Donald R. Richberg: *My Hero* (New York, 1954) and *The Rainbow* (Garden City, N. Y., 1936). Charles F. Roos was director of research for the NRA, and in *NRA Economic Planning* (Bloomington, Ind., 1937), his account of the fundamental changes in NRA economic policy benefits from his experience. Also helpful are George Terborgh, *Price Control Devices in NRA Codes* (Washington, D. C., 1934); two books by Rexford G. Tugwell: *The Battle for Democracy* (New York, 1935) and *The Democratic Roosevelt* (Garden City, N. Y., 1957); and Henry A. Wallace, *New Frontiers* (New York, 1934).

Biography

The best available biographies of key contemporaries include *J. Joseph Huthmacher, *Senator Robert F. Wagner and the Rise of Urban Liberalism* (New York, 1968); *T. Harry Williams, *Huey Long* (New York, 1969), and Thomas E. Vadney, *The Wayward Liberal: A Political Biography of Donald Richberg* (Lexington, Ky., 1970). Other biographies include *Saul D. Alinsky, *John L. Lewis* (New York, 1949); Max D. Danish, *The World of David Dubinsky* (Cleveland, 1957); Matthew Josephson, *Sidney Hillman: Statesman of American Labor* (Garden City, N. Y., 1952); and David Loth, *Swope of GE* (New York, 1958). There is a serious gap in the absence of a completed study of Hugh S. Johnson.

Background and Foreground

The memoirs and studies which relate specifically to the NRA, and are important for an understanding of its key phases, include two books by Irving Bernstein: *The New Deal Collective Bargain-*

* Available in paperback.

ing Policy (Berkeley, Calif., 1950) and **Turbulent Years: A History of the American Worker, 1933–1941* (Boston, 1970); Alfred M. Bingham and Selden Rodman, eds., *Challenge to the New Deal* (New York, 1934); Persia Campbell, *Consumer Representation in the New Deal* (New York, 1940); Charles L. Dearing et al., *The ABC of the NRA* (Washington, D. C., 1934); Sidney Fine, *The Automobile Under the Blue Eagle* (Ann Arbor, Mich., 1963); Daniel R. Fusfeld, *The Economic Thought of Franklin D. Roosevelt and the Origins of the New Deal* (New York, 1956); *J. Joseph Huthmacher, *Senator Robert F. Wagner and the Rise of Urban Liberalism* (New York, 1968); Lewis L. Lorwin and Arthur Wubnig, *Labor Relations Boards* (Washington, D. C., 1935); Charles A. Madison, *American Labor Leaders* (New York, 1950); Samuel I. Rosenman, ed., *The Public Papers and Addresses of Franklin D. Roosevelt* (13 vols., New York, 1938–50), II, *The Year of Crisis, 1933,* and III, *The Advance of Recovery and Reform, 1934;* Lester G. Seligman and Elmer E. Cornwell, Jr., eds., *New Deal Mosaic: Roosevelt Confers with His National Emergency Council, 1933–1936* (Eugene, Ore., 1965); Benjamin Stolberg, *Tailor's Progress* (Garden City, N. Y., 1944); and Norman Thomas, *As I See It* (New York, 1932).

For help in understanding the background of the times, and the key personalities involved, consult Frank Freidel's classic *Franklin D. Roosevelt* (4 vols., Boston, 1952–73), the four volumes being *The Apprenticeship, The Ordeal, The Triumph,* and *Launching the New Deal.* They are incisive and scholarly and border on the definitive for our time. Edgar E. Robinson, *The Roosevelt Leadership, 1933–1945* (Philadelphia, 1955) is often one-sided, simplistic in approach. *James M. Burns, *Roosevelt, the Lion and the Fox* (New York, 1956) is a balanced, one-volume biography. *The Great Depression, 1929–1941,* the third volume of Herbert Hoover's *Memoirs* (3 vols., New York, 1951–52), is the work of an embittered partisan. *William E. Leuchtenberg, *Franklin D. Roosevelt and the New Deal* (New York, 1963) is the best single-volume work on the subject, illustrating what can be done with original research and careful analysis in this extremely complicated field. *The Crisis of the Old Order, 1919–1933, *The Coming of the New Deal,* and *The Politics of Upheaval*—the three volumes of the monumental work *The Age of Roosevelt* (Boston, 1956–60) by Arthur M. Schlesinger,

Jr.—are brilliant, colorful, and partisan in their scholarly, favorable appraisal of Roosevelt and the New Deal. *Ellis Wayne Hawley, *The New Deal and the Problem of Monopoly: A Study in Economic Ambivalence* (Princeton, N. J., 1966) is a thorough study of business-government relations and of conflict within the New Deal administration concerning its policy on monopoly, and the first comprehensive history of the NRA. Otis L. Graham studies the role and reaction of old Progressives toward the New Deal in *An Encore for Reform* (New York, 1967). Informative, though outdated on the fiscal and economic history of the 1930s, is Broadus Mitchell, *Depression Decade: From New Era Through New Deal, 1929–1941* (New York, 1947). *Irving Bernstein, *The Lean Years: A History of the American Worker, 1920–1933* (Boston, 1960) is a vibrant account of the Great Depression. *Helen and Robert Lynd, *Middletown in Transition* (New York, 1937) is invaluable for a description of society in the 1930s. Martin Torodash, "The Blue Eagle: Government House Organ," *Journalism Quarterly,* XLVI (Spring 1969), 144–46, describes the house organ of the National Recovery Administration, the *Blue Eagle,* as given to self-praise and misuse of statistical data. Andrew D. Wolvin, "The 1933 Blue Eagle Campaign: A Study in Persuasion and Coercion," Purdue University *Dissertation Abstracts,* XXIX (February 1969) is the abstract of a Ph.D. dissertation detailing publicity for the Blue Eagle campaign in newspapers, motion pictures, radio broadcasts, and parades.

Criticism of the New Deal

Criticism by representative elements of the Old Left in the 1930s is to be found in Norman Thomas, *The Choice Before Us* (New York, 1934); Benjamin Stolberg and Warren J. Vinton, *The Economic Consequences of the New Deal* (New York, 1935); and Donald R. McCoy, *Angry Voices: Left-of-Center Politics in the New Deal Era* (Lawrence, Kan., 1958). The New Left, expanding upon but not differing fundamentally from, the critique of the Old Left, is represented in an overall appraisal by Jerold Auerbach, "New Deal, Old Deal, or Raw Deal: Some Thoughts on New Left Historiography," *The Journal of Southern History,* XXXV (February 1969), 18–30, and in Irwin Unger, "The 'New Left' and American History: Some Recent Trends in United States Historiography,"

American Historical Review, LXXII (July 1967), 1237–63. Other important New Left critiques include the "Introduction" by *Howard Zinn, ed., to *New Deal Thought* (Indianapolis, 1966); Barton J. Bernstein, "The New Deal: The Conservative Achievements of Liberal Reform," in *Barton J. Bernstein, ed., *Towards a New Past* (New York, 1968); *Paul K. Conkin, *The New Deal* (New York, 1967); and *William Appleman Williams, *The Contours of American History* (Cleveland, 1961). A slashing indictment of the NRA is found in Ronald Radosh, "The Myth of the New Deal," in *Ronald Radosh and Murray N. Rothbard, eds., *A New History of Leviathan* (New York, 1972).

Specialized Studies

William E. Leuchtenberg's essay "The New Deal and the Analogue of War," in John Braeman, Robert H. Bremner, and Everett Walters, eds., *Change and Continuity in Twentieth-Century America* (Athens, Ohio, 1964) is important for an understanding of the "cooperation" with business during the Hundred Days which significantly affected the NIRA and other New Deal legislation. Negative reactions of business spokesmen to the New Deal are detailed in Robert E. Lane, *The Regulation of Businessmen* (New Haven, Conn., 1954); George Wolfskill, *The Revolt of the Conservatives* (Boston, 1962); and Frederick Rudolph, "The American Liberty League, 1934–1940," *American Historical Review,* LVI (October 1950), 19–33. William H. Wilson, "How the Chamber of Commerce Viewed the NRA: A Reexamination," *Mid-America,* XLIV (April 1962), 95–108, seeks to modify the view of Arthur M. Schlesinger, Jr., that the Chamber of Commerce supported the NRA. James A. Hodges, "The New Deal Labor Policy and the Southern Cotton Textile Industry, 1933–1941," Vanderbilt University *Dissertation Abstracts,* XXIV (June 1964) is the abstract of a Ph.D. dissertation on the inability of the NRA boards—the Bruere Board and the Textile Labor Relations Board—to bring collective bargaining to the textile industry. Richard C. Wilcock, "Industrial Management's Policies Toward Unionism," in Milton Derber and Edwin Young, eds., *Labor and the New Deal* (Madison, Wis., 1957) shows how management's early use of strikebreakers, industrial spies, mass discrimination, and other belligerent measures was replaced, after passage of Wagner's National Labor Relations Act, by resort to state legislatures and the public media. For Congressional and state government obstruction of the New Deal, see James T. Patterson's *The New Deal and the States* (Princeton, N. J., 1969) and his *Congressional Conservatism and the New Deal* (Lexington, Ky., 1967).

Early New Deal labor policies are studied in Milton Derber and Edwin Young, eds., *Labor and the New Deal* (Madison, Wis., 1957), and a sympathetic survey is presented in *Irving Bernstein, *Turbulent Years: A History of the American Worker, 1933–1941* (Boston, 1970). Also helpful is Philip Taft, *The A.F. of L. from the Death of Gompers to the Merger* (New York, 1959). A New Left analysis of American labor is found in Ronald Radosh, "The Corporate Ideology of American Labor Leaders from Gompers to Hillman," in James Weinstein and David W. Eakins, eds., *For a New America* (New York, 1970). Charles A. Madison, "Sidney Hillman: Leader of the Amalgamated," *American Scholar, XVIII* (Autumn 1949), 457–69, views Hillman as probably the ablest leader this country has yet produced. David W. Mabon, "The West Coast Waterfront and Sympathy Strikes of 1934," University of California, Berkeley, *Dissertation Abstracts, XXVII* (September 1966) is the abstract of a Ph.D. dissertation on why the maritime strikes occurred, why they were successful, and what role the Communists played in them. According to Philip Taft, "David Dubinsky and the Labor Movement," *Labor History, IX* (Spring 1968), 26–42, Dubinsky's impact on the trade-union movement during the three decades 1935–1965, was greater than that of anyone except Lewis and George Meany. Joel Seidman, "The I.L.G.W.U. in the Dubinsky Period," *Labor History, IX* (Spring 1968), 55–68, shows how Dubinsky converted a frail organization into an effective, pioneering union. Orme W. Phelps, "The Right to Organize: A Neglected Chapter in American Labor History," in Morton J. Frisch and Martin Diamond, eds., *The Thirties: A Reconsideration in the Light of the American Political Tradition* (De Kalb, Ill., 1968), describes the exceptional service of the National Labor Board, 1933–34, in laying the groundwork for federal protection of the right to organize.

Material on the American economy in the 1930s is available in David Lynch, *The Concentration of Economic Power* (New York, 1946); *Robert Lekachman, *The Age of Keynes* (New York, 1966), on the impact of John Maynard Keynes; and Daniel R. Fusfeld, *The Economic Thought of Franklin D. Roosevelt and the Origins* *of the New Deal* (New York, 1956), on Roosevelt's economic understanding. A conservative critique of New Deal economic policy is found in *Murray N. Rothbard, *America's Great Depression* (Princeton, N. J., 1963).

Studies on specific industries include Louis Galambos, *Competition and Cooperation* (Baltimore, 1966) on the cotton-textile industry, and Gerald Nash, *United States Oil Policy, 1890–1964: Business and Government in Twentieth-Century America* (Pittsburgh, 1968). In "Experiments in Industrial Mobilization: WIB and NRA," *Mid-America,* XLV (July 1963), 157–74, Nash studies the relationship between mobilization in the First World War and in the NRA. James P. Johnson, "Drafting the NRA Code of Fair Competition, for the Bituminous Coal Industry," *Journal of American History,* LIII (December 1966), 521–41, shows that although it was neither carefully structured nor wholly viable, this code laid the foundation for marked improvement in the well-being of the miner through outlawing child labor, the company house, and the issuing of scrip.

The New Deal and the black community is the subject of John B. Kirby, "The Roosevelt Administration and Blacks: An Ambivalent Legacy," in *Barton J. Bernstein and Allen J. Matusow, eds., *Twentieth-Century America: Recent Interpretations,* 2nd ed. (New York, 1972) and Leslie H. Fishel, Jr., "The Negro in the New Deal Era," *Wisconsin Magazine of History,* XLVIII (1964–65), 111–26. *Raymond Wolters, *Negroes and the Great Depression: The Problem of Economic Recovery* (Westport, Conn., 1970) is a study of black workers and their leaders under the NRA and the AAA. *Bernard Sternsher, ed., *The Negro in Depression and War* (New York, 1969) is a useful anthology of essays. And Raymond Wolters, "Section 7a and the Black Worker," *Labor History,* X (Summer 1969), 459–74, concludes that the AF of L craft unions were hostile to the organization of black workers, and the AF of L refused to ask its member unions to end racial discrimination.

Index

188